YOU'RE OUR CHILD:
THE ADOPTION EXPERIENCE

YOU'RE OUR CHILD:
THE ADOPTION EXPERIENCE

By

Jerome Smith, Ph.D.
and
Franklin I. Miroff

Illustrations by Jill Chambers

MADISON BOOKS
Lanham · New York · London

Copyright © 1987 by

Jerome Smith & Franklin I. Miroff

Madison Books

4720 Boston Way
Lanham, MD 20706

3 Henrietta Street
London WC2E 8LU England

Printed in the United States of America

British Cataloging in Publication Information Available

Library of Congress Cataloging-in-Publication Data

Smith, Jerome.
You're our child.

Bibliography: p.
1. Adoption—United States.   2. Children, Adopted—
United States—Family relationships.   3. Biological
parents—United States—Family relationships.   4. Adoption
—United States—Psychological aspects.   I. Miroff,
Franklin I.   II. Title.
HV875.55.S65   1987   362.7'34'0973   87-16502
ISBN 0-8191-5036-2 (pbk. : alk. paper)

All University Press of America books are produced on acid-free
paper which exceeds the minimum standards set by the National
Historical Publication and Records Commission.

CONTENTS

CONTENTS

ACKNOWLEDGEMENTS

This book grew out of an effort to provide the reader with a source of information about the social and psychological dynamics inherent in the adoptive experience. There are a number of people who have contributed significantly to the production of this work.

For substantive contributions, we wish to express appreciation to the following: Terri Brassard; Aimee Hatcher; Mary Lett; Bobby Smith; Lisa Stine; and Randi Williams. For her medical and technical expertise, not only in relation to this book, but for her work in the adoptive parenting classes we offer, Deborah S. Provisor, M.D. For a truly masterful editing job, Sylvia Buck; and for the mammoth effort in programming the statistical analysis in the research portion of this book, Barbara Priest, Susan Lashmet and Ellen Gill.

Pat Stewart and Susan Metzger were helpful in the typing of the manuscript. Their individual and collective efforts typify the "going the extra mile" attitude. For the initial typing of the manuscript and to whom we are grateful for her supportive comments, the name of Patsy Branscum surfaces. Bev Myers and Ruth Hopkins also were most helpful in assisting with the typing chores.

Without the unqualified support and encouragement of Beth Carnes, former managing editor of Madison Books, this book would probably still be a dream. Wife support and encouragement in the name of Inez Smith is acknowledged with appreciation and heartfelt gratitude (at last the piles on the basement floor can be cleared away). Appreciation for support is likewise extended to M.A.H.

Finally, to our children, all of them, both adopted and biological, who provide us with the essence of living, we dedicate this book: Sandy; Bobby; Debbie; Laura and Andrew.

FOREWORD

I t is with pleasure that I respond to the request that I contribute a foreword to this book. *You're Our Child: The Adoption Experience* provides a comprehensive view of adoption processes and dynamics for all who seek an understanding of adoption: adoptive parents, couples interested in adopting, adopted children, birth parents who are confronted with choices about surrendering their child to adoptive parents, professionals working with persons who have been a part of the adoption experience, and to those who want to understand both the process and the dynamic meaning of adoption to those involved.

While the authors do a thorough job in identifying and explaining the fantasies and myths surrounding the institution of adoption and providing a clear understanding of the realities involved in the adoption process, this book does far more than that. The authors are able to convey to the reader a feeling of psychological dynamics of the process that involves the reader in an identification with each principal in the adoption triangle; the adoptive parents, the child, and the birth parents. One comes away from reading this book with a far deeper understanding of the meaning of this experience to all participants.

Written by a social worker and an attorney who are, themselves, adoptive parents, it is a unique book in that it speaks in a realistic way to the commonness of all parenting experiences and all child development struggles, while at the same time recognizing the meaning for adoptive parents and their children found in the reality that the family began through a legal process rather than a biological birth process. It deals with the meanings to the birth parent of the process of creation of a child, a releasing of the child, and facing the reality of the parting. It is unique in dealing with the birth parent's task of living with the surrender of the child, and offers us some new facts from the author's empirical research in this area.

I cannot recommend this book too highly for the professional person, social worker, attorney, doctor, judge or other professional, who works with adoption issues. This book offers an unique opportunity to develop a sensitivity to the meaning of adoption in a family's life. From reading this book professionals should come away with a realistic understanding of some of the emotional issues that an adopted child, an adoptive parent, or a birth parent must confront accepting the reality of adoption in their lives and in their relationships.

No other book so clearly introduces professionals to the meaning of adoption in family life, to adoption as an element in family functioning that adds a certain complexity to the normal family processes, neither to be denied nor overemphasized. It should be thoughtfully read by all who deal with the adoptive process.

Beulah R. Compton
University of Alabama
February, 1987.

PREFACE

This book is intended to address the concerns of the various principals in the adoption triangle: the adoptive parents, the adoptees, and the birth parents. It is in response to an observation that a comprehensive treatment of a multitude of adoption issues is currently unavailable. We hope that by focusing on the psychological tasks for all three of these groups, while at the same time, taking into account societal changes, issues and forces, a deeper understanding of what adoption really means to a child, an adolescent, a birth parent or adoptive parent, will emerge.

There are two principal reasons that this book was written. The first reason is the heartening public response to our first book on adoption. The first book, *You're Our Child: A Social-Psychological Approach to Adoption*, was written to provide adoptive parents with a guide to direct them during their child's formative and developmental years. By design, it was a skeletal framework which we knew needed further elaboration. The response to that work supported our belief that a more comprehensive work is needed, not only for the adopters, but for adoptees and birth parents as well. This current effort therefore should not be viewed as a revision of our first effort but rather a sequel to it. While we have retained the title, we have modified the subtitle to reflect the numerous changes between these two works. (A further comment on the book title will be made at the conclusion of this preface.) The second reason for writing this book is the need to identify and explain the fantasies and myths surrounding the institution of adoption. Current research and evidence are helping to dispel many of these myths. The authors feel that providing a clear understanding of the realities involved in the adoption process will assist in the development of more appropriate and realistic attitudes and behavior, and perhaps make the adjustments easier for those involved in adoption.

There are at least four main differences between these two books. In this book: (1) many actual illustrations will be used, with further analysis and interpretation; (2) attention will be directed to all parties in the adoption triangle rather than exclusively to the adoptive parents; (3) one chapter will focus on the genetic/biological aspects of adoption and another chapter will be devoted to sex education for the adoptive family; and (4) a chapter will report the findings of a rather significant piece of research, conducted by one of the authors, on attitudes of all three principals toward the sealed record controversy.

The data for the book are drawn from the personal and professional experiences of the authors, both of whom are adoptive parents. Jerome Smith is a clinical social worker-educator who is an associate professor at the Indiana University School of Social Work, Indianapolis, Indiana. He offers consultative services on adoption and related matters to various social and legal agencies in the Indianapolis and surrounding areas. He and his wife have three children, two of whom are adopted. Franklin Miroff is an attorney in private practice in the Indianapolis area who has represented numerous couples in adoption proceedings. His legal expertise in the adoption area is well established and he, too, is called upon to provide consultative services. He has two adopted children. The authors work together in providing adoptive parent counselling to new adopters and have conducted family life education courses at various sites in the Indianapolis area. It was from this joint experience that the need was initially recognized for writing the earlier book and that need continues to be recognized today.

A contemporary view of adoption today suggests somewhat of an enigma. On the other hand, there are literally thousands of children in need of permanent homes and families, literally "free" for adoption. Very few adoptive parents are interested in adopting this older, special needs child, who may be racially mixed, with an intellectual, behavioral or physical handicap, a member of a sibling group, or any combination thereof. On the other hand, there are thousands of prospective adoptive parents who desire to adopt the "blue ribbon" baby, stereotyped as a healthy white infant but whose numbers are virtually miniscule. Thus there is a very poor match between supply and demand.

As indicated earlier, the title of this book has received considerable attention. We wanted the book to reflect a comprehensive view of adoption dynamics for all three parties and set it apart from the first effort. But at the same time, we (and others) have been so enamored of the "you're our child" message that we felt some compromise should be reached. Thus the solution that has resulted is: *You're Our Child: The Adoption Experience.*

CHAPTER 1

ADOPTION—THE
CONTEMPORARY SCENE

A doption conjures up a fantasy in which a young childless couple comes to the agency, picks up their new "bundle of joy" and goes home to enjoy the pleasures of parenting. It assumes that all parties are satisfied with, if not ecstatic over, the experience. Indeed, many attorneys refer to adoption as "happy law" because there are no dissatisfied or losing parties as there are in the usual adversarial courtroom scene. It is true that adoption can be viewed as a solution to, at least, three intertwined social problems: a young girl or woman who is not ready to assume the role of parent, a child in need of a family, and an infertile couple. However, this fantasy may be only partly consonant with the reality of the situation. Research suggests that, at best, this fantasy is only two thirds true, because the birth parent, rather than experiencing joy or satisfaction regarding the arrangement, instead may experience a grief reaction of rather serious proportions. So, perhaps, adoption should better be viewed as a mixture of good and bad, pleasure and pain, fulfillment and loss.

An ecological perspective might be of some usefulness in conceptualizing the institution of adoption. The human existence does not occur in a vacuum for individuals and families. All people are somehow influenced by the trends and traditions evolving during their lifetime in the society in which they live and of which they are a part. Adoptive parents and children are no exception to this general rule. Indeed, they are uniquely vulnerable to the vicissitudes of societal attitudes toward them. The parents' success in rearing a happy and healthy child may be placed in jeopardy by the behavior of relatives, friends, neighbors, or even casual acquaintances. They are also influenced by comments made by teachers, clergy, doctors, social workers, and lawyers with whom the parents and children come into contact during their lifetime.

Even opportunities to adopt are dependent upon legal authorities, social agencies and, of course, birth parents.

The adoption picture has changed significantly over time. It seems appropriate to provide a brief historical overview so that the reader has a sense of historical perspective in understanding how the contemporary scene has evolved. Current social and economic realities have resulted in significant changes relating to adoption practices, but many seeds or elements of earlier thought and attitudes remain prevalent.

Adoption is an old social practice universally known to both simple and complex societies, with its occurrence recorded as far back as Biblical and classical times. To "adopt" comes from the Latin "adoptare" which means to consider, to look at, to choose. Historically, there have been varying views of adoption and its usefulness. For example, among the ancient Romans, adoption was viewed as a means of securing an heir in order to strengthen or extend a family line. In the Anglo-Saxon tradition, however, adoption did not exist. Neither the right to adopt nor the right to be adopted was known to English Common Law. This entire subject matter will be dealt with in greater detail in later chapters; it is sufficient to note here, however, that by the time adoption became a practice in the United States, it was purely a creation of statute (or law). Laws of adoption were introduced during the last half of the nineteenth century when the colonial practices of apprenticeship and indenture had become an inadequate provision for dependent children. There was much social change as this new nation became fully engaged in the transition from simple agrarian beginnings to an urban industrialized society. In this context, there was an increase in the incidence of child dependency, leaving the old informal solutions of close family and community ties infeasible. As a result, there emerged new forms of providing for children. Adoption represented one such new form. Having evolved from those beginnings, adoption in this country is the socio-legal process by which the parent-child relationship is established between persons petitioning to adopt and the adoptee. The subject of the petition is almost always a minor child whose ties to the birth parents have been terminated by death, abandonment, relinquishment (most frequent cause) or by court decree (least frequent cause).

Adoption has undergone changes over time. Initially, adoption was strictly a legal process and the primary concern of adoption laws was the specification of procedures that would insure the contractual integrity of the transaction. Protection of the adoptive parents' rights were of paramount importance, symbolized by the sealing of birth records and the issuance of a new birth certificate. However, the twentieth century brought an era of progressive reform and public responsibility in which protecting the health and welfare of children ranked high among social concerns. The evolution of public policy for adoption reflects the influence of this era. For the first time, the social implications of adoption were thoughtfully addressed, and efforts were started to incorporate what were seen as essential social safeguards into the laws. Adoption then evolved as a socio-legal institution and adoption law was influenced by the norms and values of social welfare and social work. In this century, it has become a child-centered institution; and the major strategies for protecting the welfare of children in adoption, as well as the interest of the other parties to the action, bear the imprint of social work ideology.

One of the earliest traditional adoption myths, no doubt partly true, revolves around an abandoned or orphaned child who needs to be rescued from desperate circumstances by a charitable couple. Reflecting the influence of the era's prevailing social Darwinistic notion of "fitness," the adoption agencies early in this century developed the concept of the "blue ribbon" baby as the only suitable child for adoption. The idea led to the unnecessary and harmful (to the child) practice of delayed placement and questionable developmental testing procedures. As recently as 30 years ago, a child would not be placed in a prospective adoptive home until he/she were at least six months of age. This was a matter of policy to insure only "high quality" placements, i.e., placements in which the baby's developmental potential matched the adoptive parent's expectations. The myth deviates substantially from the realities of today but the point is that attitudes still persist that one is rescuing a child from a life of blight and poverty. Furthermore, if the myth gets played out ("we rescued you") in the child's growth and development, the parents may well anticipate difficulties in conduct or behavioral manifestations. At any rate, it is doubtful that this myth ever truly portrayed the realities of the typical adoption, and most certainly it has nothing to do with the realities of today. There has been in recent years a sharp decline in the availability of healthy white infants for adoption. The decline has been so significant as to force social agencies, heretofore predominantly dependent on adoptive placement as principal professional service, to seek other professional service functions. As recently as ten years ago, most people hoping to adopt a child found a healthy white infant after waiting only a brief period of time. Today a couple may wait years before their name reaches the top of the waiting list maintained by an adoption agency or attorney.

Several factors contribute to this dramatic change. First, and perhaps most important, the majority of children born out of wedlock today are kept by one of the biological parents or their families. In the past an unmarried pregnant adolescent found that she had no other choice but to place the child for adoption. She now finds that keeping the child is a viable alternative. This shift in attitude is, by far, the greatest change currently affecting the adoption scene. Statistics are cited which reveal that almost nine out of ten unmarried mothers keep their babies (Zelnik and Kantner, 1978). Second, the increased use of preventive birth control measures has presumably lowered the birth rate, although there is no way of knowing how many pregnancies were actually prevented through these means. Third, the increased availability of abortion has decreased the number of children who presumably would have been placed for adoption. Finally, the decision to place or not to place may be influenced by the perceived notion in our society that many adoptees are seeking their birth parents. Certainly, one cannot guarantee anonymity and privacy in an atmosphere of public clamoring and outcry for the opening of sealed records. Hence, a birth mother may decide to either keep a child or abort in an effort to avoid such disclosures later in her life. The multiple impact of all these factors has diminished the number of children available for adoption. There is no indication whether this trend will continue or reverse itself.

Whatever the cause of this decrease in the number of children available for adoption, the effect upon adoptive parents is to eliminate the notion that they are the "rescuers." Ironically they may, instead, feel that the child rescued them from a perpetual state of childlessness. Their long waiting period provides them with ample opportunity to make a deliberate choice to be parents; however, they do not choose their baby any more than biological parents do. If anyone at all is "chosen," it is the adoptive parents, not the child.

This is not to say that the traditional rescue myth does not continue to contain a germ of truth. There remain many children awaiting adoption—older children, children with mental and physical handicaps, children with behavioral disabilities, white or biracial children of all ages and sibling groups. The adoption of these children poses substantially different problems from that of the healthy newborn of the same race as his adoptive parents.

An extended discussion of these problems and proposed solutions is beyond the scope of this book. However, the existence of these children cannot be overlooked. Couples wanting a healthy infant are advised of the availability of these other groups of children and subsequently may consider the option of adopting one of these hard-to-place children. Although most choose not to undertake this special challenge, the fact that they do consider it may contribute to a sense of having chosen their child. In this sense, adoptive parents do make a choice.

This group of "special needs" children has come to be known, not only the professionals, but to the community at large. These groups comprise a new population of children for whom adoption has become a viable option, for notable changes which reflect altered attitudes have occurred in adoption policy. Services have expanded and new concepts and principles are being applied in an effort to respond to the mandate that these children are entitled to families. The definition of "adoptable" child has changed from the healthy, attractive white infant to any child who needs and could benefit from a loving family environment. Adoptive applicants previously evaluated by standards of childlessness and economic advantage are studied for their capacity to nurture and parent. Strategies such as recruitment, reduction or waiver of fees, transracial, single parent placement and adoption subsidy are applied in the effort to achieve a more favorable balance between persons willing to adopt and children in waiting.

The contemporary scene contains other changes as well. In the past, the beginning of the parent-child relationship differed markedly from that of biological parenthood. As previously noted in this chapter, only the healthiest babies were considered adoptable, and the babies went from a maternity ward to either foster homes or institutions where they were carefully scrutinized for any possible defect. Because psychologists held the view that intelligence could be measured through the administration of infant tests, agencies delayed placement so as to avoid a situation of a poor match between the child's potential and the adopting family's expectations. Recent research evidence however, has cast doubt on the predictive value of such tests. This practice of testing has therefore been virtually abandoned. (Shyne, 1979). Research findings have altered this practice from another perspective. The findings illustrate the potential effects of psychic trauma due to recurrent shifts from one mother-figure to another. Studies show that the effects of maternal separation and possible deprivation can be minimized, if not completely avoided, when both the child and parents can establish a permanent bond of affectionate caring from the earliest possible age. The current practice of early placement of infants reflects this change of thinking. The child is released from the hospital to his adoptive parents as early as is medically permissible. Thus, the child is usually at home with his parents two or three days after birth, just as he would be if he had been born to them. His parents know as little about him as any other parent of a newborn, and they begin the parenting relationship without having to accommodate to a previous (and perhaps competitive, at least in one's fantasy) parenting style. The current practice recognizes the importance of beginning the bonding process from earliest infancy. It is advantageous to the adoptive mother, father and child because it facilitates the sense of belongingness with each other.

One of the most significant (and controversial) changes in adoption practice is referred to as "open adoption." While there are varying degrees of openness, in general "open adoption" refers to the practice of sharing identifying information (names, addresses, etc.), resulting in an erosion of the confidentiality and anonymity heretofore felt to be desirable for all parties. In some agencies the various parties meet face-to-face, and in many cases, it is the birth parents who can make the choice of prospective adoptive parents.

Those who advocate for this practice point out that the secrecy that formerly mired the adoption process and which gave rise to adoptees' anxiety about his birth parents is eliminated. The practice leaves open the prospect of face-to-face encounters between children and birth parents. Another advantage, which proponents point out, is that birth parents feel a great deal of security and control over knowing who is rearing their child. A third advantage is the opportunity to provide whatever additional data are necessary to complete a child's medical history as he continues to grow and develop. Questions which the physician raises about the child's medical history, which may or may not have been available from the previous record, can be readily answered.

However, this open adoption practice primarily benefits the birth parents, and critics of the practice point out the following: (1) the practice dilutes the process of parental entitlement, a crucial element in adoption (a concept which will be explained in great detail in chapter 3); (2) the practice complicates the process of telling the child about the adoption and may lead to considerable confusion on his part; (3) the open adoption concept paves the way for a split parental identification, the results of which are patently unclear; and (4) the practice can lead to a child attempting to play the various parental figures against each other.

There are, in addition, practical problems. For the adoptive parents, open adoption, however euphemized, reduces their role to that of caretakers. The parent-child bond, which begins with a certain fragility, and is made stronger with each passing day under a traditional arrangement, is significantly compromised. To do an effective job, adoptive parents must feel that this is their own child, not that they are filling in for the "real" parents. Adoptive parents should not be expected to wonder if the birth mother would approve of the handling of a given situation. Finally, to the extent that the birth parents are struggling with guilt over not assuming the parental role, the adoptive parents may feel that they have somehow stolen the child. This arrangement can hang over the family like a cloud that will not dissipate.

There are problems for the adopted child as well. Children need to know who are the real parents, and who carries ultimate authority over their lives. A number of questions can be asked. "What is the role of this (biological) person?" "How should I address her/him?" "Does she have to give approval for what my parents tell I should or should not do?" Do I have someone to run to for another opinion whenever I am inclined to do so?" "Does she have veto power?" "Whose family tree do I draw for my school assignment?" And most importantly, "who is my 'real' mother?" The child under an open adoption concept is more likely to develop a sense of split parental identification, —a sense much greater than would exist under the traditional practice.

Open adoption violates the very essence of sound adoption practice since there is no unconditional severing of the earlier parental ties, the legal relinquishment notwithstanding. There is still the spectre of the omni-presence of the birth parents. The open adoption practice is too new to be able to evaluate its effectiveness. Although some agencies claim that the practice is working well, it is really premature to make such a statement. The arguments made for its continued practice stem from anecdotal material and are not based on controlled, systematic, empirical data. At best, we suggest a careful analysis of open adoption to determine if its benefits outweigh its risks.

Adoption is a paradoxical phenomenon that reflects both significant changes in thinking as well as resistance to change. Even with significant changes being made in regards to some adoption issues and practices (earlier placements, controversy over open/closed records, changing perceptions of "adoptable" infants), there are other areas which continue to be very resistant to change. For example, the persistent negative reaction to the idea of adoption is portrayed in the choice of words commonly used in discussions of adoption. The historical bias is reflected in the terminology which refers to the adopted child as having "real parents" (meaning biological). Professionals, as well as lay public, exhibit this bias. In a well-known article frequently cited in adoption studies research, Marshall Schecter mentions "real parents" 17 times (1960). He reflects the societal view that biological parenthood is the more superior form, and that adoptive parents should continue to try to produce their "own child."

Examples are numerous for this bias of regarding biological parenthood as superior, a bias which we refer to as a "societal hangup with blood." Nearly every newspaper article written about Karen Quinlan in her comatose state made reference to her adoptive status. Consistently over the years, the news media continued the pattern of pointing out the adoptive status of anyone in the news. Recently, in an article on the Carruthers brother-sister team, who won a medal in the 1984 Olympics, the reporter stated: "They are an adopted brother and sister. Their adoptive parents couldn't be more proud of them if the children were 'their own.' " (Indianapolis Star, February 14, 1984).

It has been our experience in conducting classes for adoptive and prospective adoptive parents that a sensitizing process to this aforementioned bias is essential, for even among these people the term "natural parent" is frequently used as well as the term "own child," in reference to a biological child. It is necessary to help people become aware of the biased/faulty terminology they are inadvertently using so that they don't perpetuate the use of such language and the subtle messages they convey. The greatest danger of adoptive parents continuing to use such biased phrases is that children incorporate those views into their feelings about themselves. For example, in our practice it is not uncommon to hear a child refer to a person he has never met as "my real father" simply because he has incorporated this bias into his thinking. This robs both the child and the adoptive parent of the bond that is needed for sound personality development.

CHAPTER 2

HISTORY OF ADOPTION

"An Historical Perspective"

The writers on ancient law tell us that adoption is one of the oldest and most widely employed of legal "fictions" and by using this "created" bond, a "blood relationship" is established between persons who are not biologically related. The purpose of this legal tool was to prevent the extinction of the family or the clan. It was used by a large number of ancient societies and has proven to be enduring throughout the milennia.

It is perhaps difficult for us, in modern times, to appreciate the importance of the "blood relationship," but in most ancient societies, the family was the primordial group. Those who were related by blood naturally banded together for protection. Successively larger tribes joined together in the same way, based upon broader relationships. While not every early society was actually formed by a common descent from the same ancestor, all of those which achieved permanence were so descended or were deemed to be. This assumption was, of course, false since everywhere men of alien descent were admitted into families other than their own. The Greeks and Romans, for example, had adoption as a part of their society and of the law. Remember the fictional story of Ben Hur? He was adopted into a Roman family. On the other side of the world, the Japanese have also implicitly subscribed to this legal "fiction." They claim the Emperor is a descendent from the Sun in a male line "unbroken" for thousands of years.

In ancient civilizations, adoption had significant religious themes. It was carried out in a solemn rite, initiating the adoptee into a new worship and new family. The duty of the worship was the foundation of the law of adoption among the ancients. Adoption meant the complete severance of the relationship between the adoptee and his biological family and complete acceptance into the adopter's family.

Some of the earliest legal codes contain references to adoption, for example, in the 4,000 year old Code of Hammurabi (Kocourek and Wigmore, 1915):

> If a man take a child in his name, adopt and rear him as a son this grown-up son may not be demanded back.

> If a man adopt a child as his son, and after he has taken him he transgresses against his foster-father, that adopted son shall return to the house of his own father (p. 469).

The Hindus, Egyptians, and Hebrews also recognized adoption. We reveal it in the Biblical account out of Exodus about Moses in the bulrushes—Pharaoh's daughter adopted him for a son, and called him Moses, saying, "Because I took him out of the water!" In Rome, adoption was also a common practice, and we have many written accounts about its significant use.

It should be noted that there were two distinct elements of ancient adoption practices. First, the primary purpose of adoption was the continuity of the adopter's family. There was no visible concern for the "best interests" of the adoptee. The child's welfare was not deemed important at that time in our history. Second, there was the religious emphasis inherent in the practice. The adoptee was severed from the religion of his biological family and took the religion of the adopting family. The concern was the adopter's religion, with no reference to or consideration for the adoptee's prior beliefs. These two elements are relegated to a secondary consideration in modern American law.

While there is historical evidence for the practice of adoption in many cultures, it must be remembered that American legal jurisprudence was largely acquired from English common law. The practice of adoption never acquired a foothold in England because of the high regard for blood lineage. While ancient laws of adoption allowed the adoptee to become a member of the adopter's family, to acquire interest in the family's property, and to succeed to such property upon the adopter's death, the same was never true in England. In that country "heirs" meant biological children only—heirs of the blood. This was an unalterable maxim which became a fixed part of the law of the realm.

There was, therefore, no pre-modern English law of adoption. In England and America, dependent children were cared for in almshouses. They were later apprenticed or indentured, a practice tantamount to slavery. These child care alternatives were used until the mid-nineteenth century when foster parenthood was discovered as a substitute as immigration swelled our neglected child population. Strangers were accepted into English families and treated as if they were biological children. This relationship was not formalized, however, by any legal procedure, and foster children had no separate legal recognition. They were not blood heirs and could not inherit from the foster parent. In fact, adoption, as we understand it, was not legally possible in England until the Adoption of Children Act of 1926.

This is not to say that the English courts did not feel the void in the law without the law of adoption. At such times, the courts were unyielding in their presumption that a child born to a married woman was the legitimate child of her husband, no matter what the circumstances. A story is told of a child born to a married woman whose husband had been out to sea for nearly three years, and yet the child was declared legitimate by the court under its construction and interpretation of the law.

AMERICAN LAW

Since English common law did not recognize adoption, this lack of precedent impeded the institutionalization of adoption in the United States. However, once the adoption idea was incorporated into the law, our legislatures took concepts from other legal systems to form their own policy. In so doing, our courts were bound only by the terms of each particular legislative enactment.

Counted among the influences on United States adoption law are the legal systems of Spain and France. French and Spanish jurisprudence were largely modeled on Roman civil law, and because of this different historical and theoretical base, adoption was a well established practice in those countries. Those systems influenced the laws of Louisiana (France) and Texas (Spain). Therefore, there are examples of adoptions occurring in the early history of those areas long before anywhere else in the country.

The doctrine of *stare decisis* (using precedent to decide cases) and the well-known resistance of common law courts to innovations of any kind probably combined with other factors to prevent states from imitating the practices of Louisiana and Texas. Whatever the reason, adoption did not appear anywhere else in this country until specific statutes were enacted by individual state legislatures. That was a long time in coming. In fact, prior to the middle or late 1800's, if a couple wanted to adopt a child, they went to the State Legislature and got a "special bill" passed that said, in effect, "John and Mary Jones want to adopt Sam Smith" to be their child. The legislature would then pass this special bill. Another possible avenue for the couple would be to go to the Courthouse and "register" the child with the county recorder, akin to the recording of a chattel, such as a horse or a plow.

The first state to enact an adoption statute in accordance with our present concepts of the purpose of adoption was Massachusetts, in 1851. The Massachusetts statute was comprehensive, requiring assurances that the rights and needs of all parties associated therewith would be met. It proved to be a model for other states to follow, although there was wide variation from state to state.

The true origins of our adoption laws seem to lie in the concern for the welfare of children in this country beginning in the 1840's. In some respects it is directly related to changing attitudes tied to the dawning of the Industrial Revolution. As a result, the basis of our adoption laws is conceptually different from the Roman laws, in that primary concern was the welfare of the child rather than the continuity of the adopter's "house". The "best interests" formula has consistently been the cornerstone of our courts and is the distinctly American contribution to the history of the law of adoption.

Statutes and judicial interpretation today are concerned with the "best interests" of the adoptee. In fact, since the enactment of the first statute, there has been an increasing sensitivity to the manner in which the law has treated adoption. Adoption is not only a legal process which creates or alters relationships beween parties, it is also a social/psychological process. The social perspective relates to the value-laden concept of the worth of each child. The emphasis on the adoptee's well-being makes the social relationship and legal relationship interdependent.

As stated earlier, the laws of each state are the product of the legislature of that state. As a result, the nature of the law may vary. However, despite this unevenness in the drafting of the laws, the statutes of most states have a common theme. That theme is the one enunciated by the Children's Bureau some years ago. It provides for the protection of:

1. The adoptive child, from unnecessary separation from his biological family and from adoption by persons unfit to have such responsibility;

2. The biological family, from hurried decisions to give up the child; and

3. The adopting parents, by providing them information about the child and his background, and protecting them from subsequent disturbance of their relationships with the child by the biological family.

Also, because adoption laws throughout the United States are based on the "best interests" formula, there are some common issues they all address. These include questions of who may adopt and who may be adopted, when the consent of the child is necessary and when the consent of others may be necessary. The matter of inheritance by the adopted child has also been settled consistently in most states. The disposition of these and other questions have been solved with a surprising degree of uniformity from state to state.

However, even though there are similarities and common themes, prospective adoptive parents should never forget the laws of adoption in the U.S. are statutory in nature, and there are variations from state to state. It is imperative that the law be strictly followed. In other words, the only way to adopt a child in the United States is by carefully following the appropriate state statutes, for if that statute is not followed strictly, the adoption could be declared a nullity. Furthermore, there are no common law precedents to fall back on in arguing cases or supporting claims. The law was either complied with or not. If not, the adoption probably will not be legal.

THE ADOPTION PROCEDURE

Despite the fact that there is variation from state to state, there are certain commonalities, procedurally, in the adoption process. Any person may petition the appropriate court for adoption; and any person, minor or adult, may be adopted. If the adoptee is a minor, but over age 14, (some states vary this age) a written statement of his consent must accompany the petition along with the biological parents' consent. If the adoptee is under 14, the consent must be secured from both of his biological parents, if they are alive, and are, or were married. If one of the parents is dead, consent must still be acquired from the living parent. Most statutes provide for procedures for consents in the cases of children born out of wedlock and children whose parents have lost their parental rights through appropriate court action. Where a parent has abandoned the child, or cannot be located, provision is made to waive such parent's consent. This is called a consent "implied in law." The consent of the biological father in an unmarried circumstance is a major unsettled issue and law and state interpretation must be consulted to determine the need for that consent.

Upon filing of an adoption petition an investigation must be undertaken by an appropriate welfare or investigative agency. This investigation includes inquiry into the environment, family history, health history and assets of the adoptee, the home of the prospective family, stability of the family, finances and any other circumstances and conditions which might have a bearing on the desirability of adoption placement. When this investigation is finished, a report is sent to the court with a recommendation that the adoption be granted or denied.

Many states require a pre-placement investigation prior to the filing of the petition and placement of the child. This procedure covers the very same issues and concerns as discussed in the prior paragraph.

After review of the petition, the consents and evidence, the court may enter a final or interlocutory decree of adoption. No final decree of adoption may be entered unless the adoptee shall have been living with the petitioner for a minimum period of time as prescribed by the statute or by local court rules.

For the most part, all proceedings, records and papers with reference to adoption are deemed confidential. No one may inspect the records or papers except upon the order of the court and then only for "good cause." Thus, total termination of the adoptee's ties with his biological family is effectuated except for possible intestate inheritance. Some states have "open records" which allow inspection upon the attaining of adulthood. There are many variations on this theme—some with requirement of consent of biological parents, adoptive parents and court prior to opening of records. (This is but another adoption issue in a state of flux and will be dealt with extensively in chapter 12.) In the matter of inheritance between adopter-adoptee, adoptee-biological parents and both sets of collateral relatives, adoption law in the United States has not always been consistent. This has been caused by the relationship of the adoption statutes and the general probate provisions on inheritance. The descent and distribution statutes are regarded as controlling by the courts unless clearly and expressly changed by the adoption laws. The law in the particular jurisdiction should be checked to determine if there is a "cut off" for purpose of inheritance when a child is adopted.

ADOPTION, RELIGION AND THE LAW

While adoption procedures are fairly straight forward, one element can complicate the process, and that is religion. It derives from a concern for the child's spiritual welfare and is a component of the "best interest" formula.

There are two reasons which have been offered stating that religious belief should never be considered a proper issue in a civil court of the United States. The first is that our courts have no heritage of ecclesiastical precedent to turn to for guidance. We specifically rejected the common law notion that acknowledge the spiritual jurisdiction of the English ecclesiastical courts. Because of this, if we were to include religion as a major element of the process, then our judges could examine only their own individual religious beliefs for guidance in deciding issues which involve spiritual elements. There would be no body of law to guide them. To allow reliance on this personal bias is anathema to our concept of an impartial judiciary.

The second offered reason derives from a strongly developed historical sense of the impropriety of submitting religious issues to legislative or judicial determination. Our Bill of Rights has always been a barrier to our legislatures and our courts delving into the church-state issues.

In spite of these historic legal reasons for religious nonintervention, many states have enacted laws which make religious belief a consideration in the judicial determination of adoption.

Courts have usually refused to consider religious belief as a *controlling* factor unless the welfare of the child was equally well secured by those competing for his custody or adoption. The statutory directive tips the scale only when all of the interests are in balance. In reality, as a practical observation, most courts would probably place exactly the same emphasis on religious belief even without statutory authority.

These decisions, although sound in principle, avoid the fundamental controversy lying dormant within these statutes. Prospective adoptive parents need to be aware of this possible complication, and check out the law and the rulings in their home state.

INTERSTATE ADOPTIONS

Another possible complication adoptive parents need to consider lies in the area of interstate adoptions. In 1980, the Montana Supreme Court ordered a child removed from the home of a prospective adoptive couple and returned to the birth mother. The court apparently did not consider evidence of the couple's suitability as adoptive parents, but merely the evidence of the failure to follow procedures mandated by the Interstate Compact on the Placement of Children.

Placing a child for adoption into a state that has enacted the Interstate Compact, without full compliance with the Compact prior to or contemporaneous with the actual placement with the adoptive family, would probably be a violation of the laws of both the sending and receiving states. Currently the Interstate Compact on the Placement of Children is a statutory law in more than forty states. When both states have enacted the Compact, a signed Interstate Compact Agreement is required for each placement for adoption. The law of the sending states must be consulted because some states have laws which complicate or prohibit independent, nonagency adoptions.

In most states, appointment of a guardian *ad litem* for the child is required for an adoption within the state. The term "guardian ad litem" designates the person who is appointed to represent the interests of the child in a specific litigation. With increasing attention given to children's rights, such protection has become much more common. The Interstate Compact, however, requires *appointment of a "full" guardian of the person of the child*, rather than a guardian *ad litem*. The court appointed guardian cannot be the child's parent; nor can it be the prospective adoptive family.

The guardian of the person must be willing and able to assume ultimate planning and financial responsibility for the child until the final decree has been entered. The guardian's responsibilities are wide and varied, and include care and maintenance of the child. If re-placement is necessary due to the failure to consummate the adoption, the guardian is responsible for paying all costs of the care, and returning the child to the sending state.

The order which terminates the parental rights should appoint an individual as guardian of the person and should specify that the guardian has the power to consent to the child's adoption. Compliance with the Compact requires that the original court order on the guardianship clearly states that the court's jurisdiction over the child shall continue until the child is legally adopted.

The prospective adoptive family must make arrangements with a licensed agency—with a private public child welfare agency—for an adoptive home study prior to placement. They must also arrange for post placement supervision (usually by the same agency) during the period after entering of the Interim Order, while the child is in their custody. The laws of the receiving state must be consulted regarding specific preplacement requirements.

The Compact Office in the sending state reviews the Request for Placement and all the court orders and documents. If the sending state's statutes and rules are properly met, the Request for Placement is forwarded to the receiving state's Compact Office for review. When that office has also received the adoptive family's home study recommendations, and licensing, if required by that state, the receiving state will authorize placement by returning the Request for Placement form to the sending state's Compact Office. The signed Interstate Compact form authorizing placement is then provided to the court in the receiving state. When the court also receives the final report from the agency supervising the adoption, the process can be completed. When the Compact Office in either the sending or the receiving state receives the final order of adoption, the office in both states close their files and the adoption is completed. If state laws have been violated or not followed by not fully complying with the Compact, it may be impossible to retroactively comply. Prospective parents should make sure they have proper legal advice in order to complete the transaction.

ADOPTION OF HARD TO PLACE CHILDREN

In the past, many children were unadoptable because they required expensive medical care or other services that few adoptive parents could afford, or because the foster parents appeared to be the best caretaker but were unable to forego ongoing foster care payments. These barriers have been alleviated somewhat by the passage of adoption subsidy statutes. These statutes will, among other things, provide federal matching payments for state adoption subsidy programs. However, states retain significant discretion whether to grant a subsidy, as well as to set the amount. There may be resistance by the State in private placement situations to the granting of these subsidies. The State statutes should be consulted by prospective parents willing to consider this adoption alternative.

ADOPTING FROM FOREIGN COUNTRIES

As a result of the decreased availability of adoptable infants from within the United States, there has been a great increase in the last several years of foreign-born children adopted by U.S. citizens. Intercountry adoptions is indeed a viable alternative for childless couples, but it can also be a complex, frustrating experience if the couple is not prepared for the necessity of meeting regulations of several layers of government. Foreign countries differ widely in their legal processes for intercountry adoption, and they maintain different requirements for adoptive parents. The process can take anywhere from a few months to a year or longer.

Generally, intercountry adoptions fall into two categories—1) those processed by U.S. based intercountry adoption agencies that help facilitate adoptions here and abroad, and 2) "direct" or parent initiated adoptions in which adopting parents usually have the primary role and responsibility for locating the child and expediting the adoption.

Asian countries generally favor adoptions through U.S. based international agencies. In such adoptions, the agency is responsible for identifying and caring for children, legally freeing them for adoption, selecting adoptive families, and processing families and children so that the parties can be united. The agency, then, usually brings the child to the United States for placement with specified families. In most cases guardianship of the child is held by the agency of foreign government for a six month trial period after which consent is issued. Travel to the foreign country by the adoptive parents is usually not required.

Latin American countries prefer direct adoptions over the agency facilitated adoptions. With direct adoptions, the parents make contacts with orphanages or intermediaries in foreign countries. When they have been informed about a child, one or both parents must travel to the country in which the child lives to finalize the adoption according to that country's laws. The parents may then return to the United States with their child. Since adoptions consummated in foreign countries are recognized by approximately only two-thirds of our states, a re-filing of the papers in the state of the parents' residence is good practice.

The United States Immigration and Naturalization Services requires adoptive parents to obtain an "orphan" visa for the child to be admitted to the United States. Before the visa can be issued, a U.S. Immigration officer investigates to assure that the child is irrevocably free for intercountry adoption. In addition, the adoptive parents must be certified by authorities in their state of residence as having met all preadoption requirements.

To meet the state preadoption requirement, an adoptive home study must be conducted by a licensed child placement agency. Some states also have regulations involving proof of child's eligibility for adoption, temporary guardianship, and posting bonds during the adoption process.

Proof of satisfaction of all state preadoption requirements must be submitted to the Immigration and Naturalization Service, which will then take action on the visa application and forward its decision to the appropriate American embassy or consulate abroad, resulting in the issuance of the visa. The visa is issued when the child is ready to travel pending issuance of passport or exit visa by the government of the child's home country.

The intercountry adoption agencies provide most or all services in the U.S. and abroad to effect immigration of the children to the United States. Parents choosing to go the "direct" adoption route ordinarily complete all steps themselves or locate individuals who can assist them.

After the child arrives in the United States, steps can then be made to finalize the adoption in a U.S. court or reconfirm the adoption through a second adoption hearing. After the adoption has been finalized, the child is eligible to become a naturalized U.S. citizen. Parents work directly with the Immigration and Naturalization Service in this final step.

Once the child has become a naturalized U.S. citizen, it is advisable for the adoptive parents to check with authorities in the child's home country to learn whether a process to nullify the original citizenship exists. If this step is not taken, and when the child enters that country after becoming an adult, technically he or she could be inducted into military service or held in that country. (The child could be a "dual citizen".)

CHAPTER 3

ENTITLEMENT: CONCEPT AND PROCESS

A doption is a multi-faceted creation. It is a social invention designed to give permanence to a parent-child relationship between individuals who are not so related biologically. Adoption, well carried out, gives a child lasting parental images with which to identify. He develops normally within a relationship with his parents, a relationship in which he receives a good measure of those ingredients necessary for sound personality growth. It is the love and acceptance which will form the basis for stability and productivity in later life. Being wanted gives a child the sense of desirability and worthiness; but being adopted is a legal contract as well, signifying a relationship binding together three individuals who have, in a real sense, chosen each other.

Adoption is both a beginning and an ending. It is a beginning of a life-long relationship in which two adults voluntarily assume the rights and privileges of a parent, rights which have to do with caring, nurturing, disciplining and worrying. Being a parent means being totally committed to the health and well being of your child for life. At the same time, it is an ending. The adoption signifies a termination of the parental rights of those responsible for the child's birth. Typically, the termination precedes the adoption, although frequently these two legal procedures occur simultaneously.

Adoptive parenthood is similar to biological parenthood in many ways. After final approval of the adoption petition, the child becomes the child of the adoptive parents just as if he had been born to them. The adoptive parents assume the responsibility for care and welfare of the child, who becomes an integral part of the family. The adoptive parents relate to the child with all the love and care they would invest in their biological child.

However, it is important to be aware of the differences between adoptive and biological parenthood. Most of the differences derive from the fact that the child came to the family by a different route. Consequently, the societal view regarding parenthood comes into play in a different way. The societal presumption is that the best parents for any given child are his biological parents, and this presumption gets played out in a multiplicity of ways. If the question of "fitness" of the individuals to be parents arises, in the case of biological parents, society must prove that they are incapable or unwilling to be suitable parents. On the contrary, adoptive parents bear the burden of proof to society that they are capable of being good parents. From this overall distinction derive a number of differences. First, biological parents need no intermediary to become parents, whereas adoptive parents require either a social agency or an attorney or both to intercede in their behalf. Biological parents know from the outset that the child is unconditionally theirs. Adoptive parents, on the other hand, are first faced with uncertainty about whether they will receive a child. Even after the adoption process is underway, they maintain an uneasy tentativeness about the permanency of the arrangement. They worry about some last minute legal maneuvering that will result in their loss of the child. Despite the improbability that the child will be removed during the supervisory period by the agency or court, fear and apprehension haunt many adoptive parents until the adoption is actually approved in court.

There are other procedural differences as well. Biological parenthood is presumed to become a reality within a predictable period of time, giving the family an opportunity to prepare emotionally for the arrival of the child while prospective adoptive parents are never completely certain whether and when to expect the child. It is, in fact, a nerve-racking experience to prepare, psychologically, for an event which may, in reality, never come to pass. When a couple finally does get word of the birth of the child who is to be theirs, there is often such a flurry of activity in making the necessary arrangements that it may be some time before they feel the joy of receiving the child.

In addition to facing the differences relating to societal views and resulting procedures for the two types of parenthood, adoptive parents have unique psychological hurdles to clear before they can come to terms with the "realness" of their parenthood. Their situation leads to certain feelings which are virtually inevitable.

We refer to the feelings of parental rightfulness to the child as "entitlement." The sense of entitlement of the parents to child, of child to parents, and siblings to each other is a task unique to adoption. Entitlement is related, but not identical, to the resultant feelings of belongingness. There are both intellectual and emotional components to entitlement and belongingness which may take some time to develop. For the family who has achieved both of these tasks, i.e., entitlement and belongingness, the perception is solid that the child is unconditionally (and exclusively) their own child. This is a relatively easy procedure in having a biological child and usually occurs at an unconscious level. For adoptive parents, however, there is this extra psychological step involved.

Every adoptive parent and every adopted child has to come to terms with the question of: "Who are the 'real parents' "? Are they the ones who begot the child or are they the ones who give the child love and nurturance? This question can have critical impact for both parents and the child. It has been our experience in counseling countless adoptive couples that the child incorporates the parents' attitude on this issue. If the parents have worked through their feelings about the "real parents," so will the child—and vice versa. One adoptee stated the distinction between birth and adoptive parents in this way: "Your parents are not the ones who gave you your genes—your parents are the ones who gave you your love." According to this view, and this person's interpretation of adoption, there are not two sets of parents—distinction is made between parents and the persons who begot the child.

A biblical note on this issue is that in the Judeo-Christian tradition, the parents are identified as the ones who fulfill the caring, nurturing role. The definition of the Talmud, (the moral and legal text of rabbinic Judaism), identifies the father as the one who raises the child, not as the one who gave birth. A full discussion of the Jewish position on adoption is not the intent of this book. However, we feel a need to note that while a disproportionate number of adoptive families are Jewish, most children placed for adoption are not Jewish by birth. And since Judaism defines Jewish status on the basis of the birth mother's religion, adoptive parents may wish to discuss conversion with their rabbi as part of the adoption process. One should recognize, also, that variations exist within Judaism. Procedurally, entering into the "covenant" varies according to whether the family is of Orthodox, Conservative, Reconstructionist or Reform persuasion.

Entitlement is an extremely complex phenomenon and there is some evidence to suggest that it is not a question of whether or not one feels entitled, but to what degree the sense of entitlement has been developed. A partial sense of entitlement may manifest itself in certain areas: problems of discipline; difficulty with allowing the child a measure of independence and individualization from the parents; or difficulty discussing the adoption. It may also manifest itself in feelings of guilt about the fact that the child may never access full knowledge in regard to his genetic past. A child's behavior problems may remind some parents of their infertility, resulting in overreactions of either rejection or overprotection. As parent-child conflicts become more unmanageable, the parent may wonder if such behavioral difficulties are characteristic of all children at that age, or if they are attributable in some way to the adoption. Such adoptive parents are vulnerable because the uneasy feeling that the child is not really "theirs" interferes with their ability to exert appropriate authority. In a study of adoptive mothers, clinicians discovered that most of the mothers felt that they somehow did not have a right to the child (Walsh and Lewis, 1969).

Often the only way to tell if a parent is struggling with issues of entitlement is by inference. Adults have an unusual capacity for self-deception and denial. Hence, the inquiry: "Do you feel this is your own child?" invariably yields a positive response: "Oh, yes, without question." Subsequent questioning, however, often reveals that the initial response was strictly an intellectual one, devoid of self-understanding and insight. The parents may, in further discussion, relate concerns indicative of guilt feelings in regard to disciplining the child. They may admit to becoming defensive when outsiders compare the appearances of the adopted children and parents. They also may reveal feelings of anxiety in discussing adoption with others. What these signals may mean is that the process of dealing with the entitlement issue continues to be problematic. Parents need to examine their own views and feelings, and perhaps even seek professional help in this regard.

The overall task of achieving a sense of entitlement is best accomplished through the achievement of certain subtasks. The first is to recognize and accept the differences between the two different forms of parenthood. Adoption experts agree that acknowledgement of differences will result in more relaxed communication between parents and child and hence, a better adjustment to the adoptive situation. Various studies which examined the connection between orientation to acknowledgement of differences (versus rejection of differences) and relationship capability found there was a positive association between the two. Those couples who accepted their child's different origins scored significantly higher on relationship capability than those couples who rejected such differences. A second necessary subtask of achieving a sense of entitlement is to recognize and deal with feelings attendant to infertility. Adults whose sense of personal competence is not contingent upon biological reproduction can do this without evoking feelings of inadequacy. The third subtask is to handle the myriad of questions and comments about the child's adoptive status—comments which reflect the societal view that biological parenthood is superior to adoptive parenthood. A fourth subtask is involved for many people. It is to overcome feelings of guilt and sadness regarding the birth mother's anguish at giving up her child. The joy of becoming parents is lessened by the sense that their joy is at someone else's expense. The result may well be some tentativeness about their feelings of rightfulness to the child.

For many prospective adoptive parents, the first and most difficult of the subtasks to achieving a sense of entitlement involves the understanding and working through of their strong emotional reactions to infertility. Psychic pain stems from at least two sources: (1) The perception that infertility is a threat to one's image as a sexual adult; and (2) the perception that the inability to conceive and/or carry a fetus to full-term is a major personal failure. Most people grow up with a fantasy that they will produce a child which will, for better or worse, mirror their own lives in a variety of ways and therfore, perpetuate their own sense of immortality. For some, the sense of personal competence as an "okay" human being is inextricably tied up with reproductive capacity. The inability to conceive represents a major narcissistic injury. It is necessary for adoptive parents to come to terms with their infertility by mourning the loss of their reproductive capacity as well as the inability to anticipate a child by birth.

We can think of several situations in which the entitlement issue was a definite problem. In this first case, the adoptive mother was reflecting on her feelings at the time of placement:

> In the beginning I always wanted Tami to like me. I don't know
> why but I guess I was afraid that she would reject me. Because
> of my age, I thought she would look at me and say "Why did
> you adopt me? You could have left me there until someone
> else (younger) came along." That fantasy haunted me over the
> years and made me wonder what right I had to adopt her.

In this situation, we have a 13 year old adoptee, Tami, who
is simply ungovernable and who runs the household as she sees
fit. Any rules that the parents attempted to lay down are ignored
and scorned by Tami. In the interview situation, she denied that
she had any feelings for her parents. She denied that she lived
in a family, and instead referred to living "only with some people in a home."

It became obvious to the therapist that not only did the adoptive mother not feel a right to Tami, but that Tami felt she could
best protect her need to maintain this emotional distance by refusing to become involved with the family. This distancing
mechanism protected Tami, already once "burned" by the abandonment by her birth mother, from being hurt again. The lack
of entitlement worked both ways.

In another case, Mr. and Mrs. M. had been married for five
years, and had one biological child when they received the news
that they would never have another. Mrs. M. began to sob, where-
upon the physician advised her to contact the XYZ agency immediately to initiate adoption proceedings. An infant was placed
with Mr. and Mrs. M. within a matter of weeks. Years later the
(adopted) child manifested many behavioral problems. The
following is an excerpt from a meeting which she and her husband had with one of the authors:

Dr. S.:   "Do you feel that you have to compete with this other
          woman?"

Mrs. M.: "The other mother? Absolutely. She was a threat to
          me from day one. Becuase I know how I feel about
          Raymond (my biological child), and I know how I feel
          about that birth connection, even though a lot of peo-
          ple in the group (of adoptive parents that had met
          several nights before) stated that there is no difference."

Mr. M.: "Don't forget that a lot of those parents' kids are too young to know what adoption is in the first place. Of course they don't have troubles yet—their kids aren't even at the talking stage."

Mrs. M.: "But I'm afraid. You know, I saw myself getting out there on that proverbial limb. I find myself getting these attacks of anxiety because there are things I want to say but I'm terrified to say them."

Dr. S.: "What would you like to say?"

Mrs. M.: "I wanted to say, 'I don't know how many of you sitting in this room have done it both ways. There is a difference and don't let anyone tell you otherwise. I don't have to worry about our own child, but for our adopted child, I'm scared that she is going to run away when she is 16. I'm scared that she is going to look for her [birth mother]."

Mr. M.: "I guess we're all worried about that."

Mrs. M.: "I'm terrified of that. I'm afraid of being judged. I'm afraid of her having to make a choice between two mothers, one who has made a lot of mistakes and some terrific mothers who never made any."

Dr. S.: "You know, she's going to have to find herself, no matter what."

Mrs. M.: "I know."

Dr. S.: "Maybe you're not seeing things realistically because your feelings are obscuring the reality. But when I spoke to your daughter the other day, there was no question in my mind that she feels she belongs to you. Now I don't know for sure if that was just a put-on or if she really understood the depth of my question, but I think she did. You're her parents. She knows that intellectually. But its been a garbled kind of message. I hate to keep throwing up the nature of the message, but its very important. What I mean is that if you're still competing with that woman out there, how are you going to demonstrate to your child that you're her mother if that competition is still brewing? The thing

29

is—when you look at her, do you say, "You're my child?"

Mrs. M.: "Oh, absolutely. I always have. I mean it, I've never thought of her as being anything other than ours— mine, but on the other hand, I have to qualify that a little bit. I don't ever forget. I remember it, it's part of what she is. I remember that. You see, to me I guess that's where my ambivalence comes from. That's part of her identity. She is adopted. That's what she is. To say that she isn't, or to forget about it is foolish."

Mr. M.: "But I do. I mean, I've said to Jane—and never thought a thing about it at the time—Jane, you're a little fuss-budget, like your Grandma Miller. You're just fussing around all the time."

Mrs. M.: "I've said those things too, because those are her grandparents."

Dr. S.: 'That's good."

Mrs. M.: "Okay, and I believe that. Those are her grandparents, they are the only grandparents we know anything about, or she knows anything about, but nevertheless, to forget it is senseless. She is adopted and one of the most pointed ways that we could ever even bring that subject up had to do with her name. I want her to have that."

Dr. S.: "I don't understand."

Mr. M.: "She was given the name, Miriam, by her biological mother."

Mrs. M.: "We had not picked out a name for her. When we went to get her that morning, a caseworker came out and was giving us background information and told us that the biological mother was 17 years old, said goodbye to her baby, and asked that this name be given to her. That's part of what makes it so hard for me. Because I do identify with her birth mother, and know how hard it is to do—to give up that baby she carried for nine months, to know that somebody you're never going to see is going to drive up in a car and take this baby away from you, and that's it. It had to be devastating to her. And so we felt right then that we would honor her request and had it told to her. So that's why her middle name is Miriam."

Mr. M.: "That's the way it happened. But I would have never felt the need to keep that name. Why should we?"

Mrs. M.: 'I felt like we had been put through an ordeal, but that somebody was, out of their own pain, making up to us and giving us her baby. Anyway, when it comes right down to it, I don't think we have any right to her. That's why everytime I see a TV show in which the birth mother shows up and says, 'I want my baby back,' it makes me so angry and so confused. I feel badly for both mothers. I mean, who does have the right?"

Dr. S.: "It sounds to me like tremendous demands were placed on the two of you in caring for this baby. While I don't want to be critical of the caseworker, it's evident to me that a message was being given to you that the birth mother had a most difficult time in letting go. So your feelings of anguish, confusion and guilt are quite natural and I'm glad you got them out in the open."

Mrs. M.: "When I've really been horrible to Jane, I think about this 17 year old girl, and I think about what if she knew?"

Dr. S.: "What if she knew what?"

Mrs. M.: "What if she knew that I treated this baby so badly? What if she wanted to come and take her away from me?" (Sobs).

Dr. S.: "Are you feeling that you somehow stole the baby?"

Mrs. M.: "Sort of."

Dr. S.: "But the reality is that you did not steal or kidnap Jane. Whatever you have done to or for her, you've done in the name of wanting her to be the kind of person you believe she ought to be. Nobody said you had to be perfect. I would suggest that you examine your real feelings toward Jane and ask yourself if they would be any different if she were your biological child. But we place an inordinate standard of parental perfection on adoptive parents because of our belief that blood ties are everything."

Mrs. M.: "I have that hangup with blood."

Dr. S.: "Well, you're part of our culture."

This case illustrates certain points: (1) Mr. and Mrs. M. did not have time to grieve the loss of their reproductive capacity; (2) they were ill-prepared for differences between biological and adoptive parenthood; (3) Mrs. M. felt unusually competitive with the birth mother; and (4) the fact that M's awareness of the difficulty the birth mother had in severing her ties with the child left the M's with a precarious uneasiness about their rights to the child. Obviously, the M family had not successfully worked through the issue of entitlement. Some aspects of their problems might have been alleviated by working through the feelings surrounding infertility and the differences between adoptive and biological parenthood. If that was not sufficient, it would be best for Mrs. M. to seek professional help in order to resolve her feelings and foster her sense of entitlement.

There are varying, though strikingly familiar, theoretical models explaining characteristic phases which couples go through before the resolution of painful feelings can be considered to be complete. One is the work of Elisabeth Kubler-Ross, whose development of the mourning process is particularly helpful in understanding how couples deal with the impact of infertility (1969). These phases of mourning entail an extremely lengthy process which cannot be rushed. For adoptive parents, an understanding of these phases is imperative.

There is ample evidence to suggest an identifiable association between resolution of infertile feelings and family functioning. Unresolved feelings of disappointment, anger, or guilt concerning infertility can have a powerful effect on family life. Infertility may be perceived as a deprivation or even as a loss. Failure to come to grips with such feelings may result in an atmosphere of tension for the adopted child and the family as a whole. Elizabeth Lawder's research (1969), in which she examined the relationship between adoptive outcome and attitudes toward infertility, suggests that the ability of the father and mother to accept infertility does have a bearing on the acceptance of the adopted child and hence, on the child's later functioning. She states:

> The adoptive mother's ability to discuss infertility prior to placement was significantly related to outcome. Although the father's ability to discuss infertility showed a relationship to parental functioning, the degree of relationship was consistently smaller than that from the mother . . . the association between the mother's ability to discuss infertility and parental communication of the fact of adoption to the child suggest that the better the parents understand these feelings the better they are able to cope with the related problem of telling the child of his adoption (p. 167).

Again, we need to stress that it is not the fact of infertility that is the critical variable, but the resulting feelings about having missed the opportunity to take an active part in the biological procreative process.

Actually, our knowledge of how couples react to the news of childlessness is rather sparse and has come from limited data. In general, however, the reaction can be likened to a reaction to any severe crisis. There are a number of phases characteristic of the process families go through in accepting the fact of infertility. Couples typically go through these phases, even though the phases vary in length and tend to overlap with each other (Mazor, 1979). The phases consist of (1) a period of denial; (2) anger and grief reactions; and (3) acceptance.

During the first phase, many couples deal with their feelings of disappointment by denying the reality of the situation. A characteristic response is "not us." In order to prove the fallacy of their fears, many couples go through a number of medical procedures and tests, some of which are physically painful and some of which are psychologically demeaning. Some people react with a sense of helplessness at losing control over their life's plans. It has been our experience that people who truly value their own autonomy and sense of control over their lives experience considerable difficulty in accepting the reality of this one "flaw." Other individuals may go through a bargaining phase during this period, in which they offer to suffer in return for a baby. Such bargaining is exemplified in the biblical account of Hannah, who promised to give her son (if God granted her wish) to the Lord all the days of the child's life (1 Samuel 1:11).

During the second phase, denial is replaced by anger as the couple now asks "Why us?" The couple may feel an extreme sense of injustice as if they had somehow been singled out for this problem. Couples may question which partner is "at fault" and begin to doubt the security of their marriage. The experience leads the individuals to feel a sense of failure. Even couples whose relationship is good and whose marriage is strong may experience these feelings of insecurity and failure, at least temporarily. A typical comment by one spouse to the other is "If you had married someone else, you would have a child by now." The feeling that one has betrayed the bloodline, as well as the spouse, is difficult to counteract.

In part, this reaction is linked to our folklore, and in our experience it is more likely to involve the woman. One frequently heard remark is, "You're not a woman until you have had a baby." In addition, in our culture at least, women are considered to be the adult family member most responsible for the maintenance of family ties. While there is some indication of changing societal values with men and women sharing this responsibility, the prevailing attitude still seems to be that men are primarily responsible for maintaining the family indirectly through their work or professions, while women are ordinarily viewed as the carriers of the responsibility for maintaining family ties within the home. Another reaction, culturally derived, is the feeling that one does not deserve to enjoy sex since a baby is not being produced. Again, this derives from sexual mythology which states that the sole purpose of sex is to procreate. This perspective is changing, but there is always a time lag between changing ideologies and our inculcation of them.

Grief and mourning, as well as the anger, are experienced with considerable intensity during the second phase. Many couples report, however, that the mourning experience during this phase has brought them closer than before. For the couple able to acknowledge such feelings, there follows a desire to handle them through discussion with each other or professional counseling. Feelings of inferiority can be alleviated by restoring confidence in parental capacity, by a hope that one can continue to satisfy the partner emotionally, and by a recognition that sexual competence and reproductive powers are not synonymous. It is important to recognize that this is a process of working through feelings over a period of time, and that old feelings (of inferiority, failure, and incompleteness) are not easily dissipated. One must keep comparing the emotional feelings with the intellectual understanding of the situation, and occasionally ask oneself "What is the reasonableness of this feeling (of inadequacy or inferiority) and to what extent is it tied to the reality of the situation?" The answer may be a long time in coming. The main thing to remember is that it does involve *a process*, a working through of feelings, and that mutual supportiveness of husband to wife and vice versa, regardless of who is "at fault," is essential.

Some couples may feel themselves "stuck" in the anger phase. For infertile couples, the anger is most frequently a response to the helplessness and loss or control over life's plans, hopes and goals. In an effort to regain control, many couples become preoccupied with the timing of sexual activity to coincide with the period of anticipated ovulation. The desperation and artificiality associated with sexual activity often are unrecognized sources of anger for those couples who heretofore enjoyed sexual spontaneity (Shapiro, 1982). As the concern of sexual intercourse shifts from pleasing the partner and self to the fertilization of the ovum, or the process to results, feelings of hopelessness and anger inevitably result. Many couples learn to avoid love-making in the spirit of it not being the "right time," and indeed, many experience a loss or weakening of the sex drive itself.

A period of depression sets in when the couple realizes that no amount of diagnostic workups, regardless how specialized they may be, no surgical intervention, and no amount of bargaining will change the basic fact: there is a high degree of improbability that pregnancy will occur. Together, the couple must come to terms with the loss of their reproductive powers and mourn the fantasied loss. It is truly a difficult task because the loss is so vague—there is no formal funeral ritual to acknowledge the loss. It is also difficult because people can be quite insensitive to the pain experienced—some even to the point of joking about the fun to be experienced in trying again. The loss may be mourned again on many occasions, for the world is full of reminders that other people continue to have babies, but the pain becomes less acute with the passage of time. In a sense, learning to live with infertility is akin to learning to live with the reality of death—it is part and parcel of the life experience itself.

The final stage of working through the feelings is acceptance. This stage is characterized by coming to terms with the nature of the situation with which they are faced. This presumes an attitudinal stance in which the couple realizes that while they may not propagate children in a biological sense, life is full of rewards and satisfactions. However, during this stage, there may be renewed desire for a child, and the compensatory wish to give of oneself (to a child) becomes stronger. Finally, couples who cannot procreate realize that they can find enormous satisfaction and fulfillment in contributing to a child's growth and development even if that child is not "born" to them in a physical sense. It is not procreation which makes one a parent, but the sense that one is contributing meaningfully to the life and self-actualization of another human being. Of utmost importance to the couple's ability to achieve a comfortable level of acceptance is their ability and willingness to share feelings with each other and to recognize that their feelings are natural and normal.

Couples should be aware of their feelings regarding infertility so that unresolved feelings will not result in problems with family relationships and family functioning. How does a couple know when they have resolved such feelings? In general, an ability to discuss adoption openly, a tendency to answer questions regarding the adoption without defensiveness or resentment, and an ability to discuss adoption with the child at appropriate times are indications of a relatively healthy resolution.

It is relatively easy to detect failure in resolution. Some of the many possible indications are: prolonged denial of feelings of disappointment; sadness or resentment in observing a pregnant woman; reacting with annoyance or irritation to "normal" children's play; avoidance of family reunions where children are expected to be present; obsessive fears that the child will not measure up to family standards; anxiety about discussing adoption; repeated joking remarks about the similarity between the child's and (adoptive) parents' looks and/or behavior; bringing up the child's adoption under virtually any circumstances; feeling compelled to tell the child how the parents "took him in" at varying points in the child's life (the rescue notion); fantasies about one's imagined biological child; a persistent, nagging feeling about having been cheated, leading to a "not fair" response; and unabating resentment toward visits by the agency social worker.

While this list is not exhaustive by any means, it is somewhat representative of the kinds of situations reflecting gross uneasiness about feelings related to infertility and hence, adoption. Some of the responses fall into the denial category; others fall into the angry or "why us?" category. We feel it important however, that adults *be aware of their feelings*, irrespective of their irrationality, and be prepared to discuss them either with one's spouse or a professional mental health clinician.

Because of the stigma generally associated with mental health counseling, many people are loathe to seek it out. The need to make use of such services should not be interpreted as a perceived defect in one's psychological armor. There are two types of assistance available. Individual counseling by one trained in helping couples deal with the special psychological tasks can lead to a greater sense of entitlement. In many cases, this involves a working through of feelings which previously blocked a healthier adjustment. Groups on adoptive parenting can also be helpful. Groups are valuable ways of satisfying a natural desire for group belonging. Group discussions provide a means by which parents can talk about and reveal the myriad ways in which each couple deals with life and growth problems. Besides revealing problems, the group discussions demonstrate how gratifying the trying out of new experiences has been and how their lives have changed. It is necessary to know that there are others who also struggle with the special problems preparatory to adoptive parenthood, and it is comforting to see that these struggles do not make them poor parents or any less the parents of their children.

There is a practical matter to be considered in the timing of adoption inquiries and application. In the past, it has been our advice to counsel people not to adopt until they have, more or less, successfully dealt with their feelings surrounding their childlessness. This was good advice when healthy babies were plentiful and the wait was relatively short. But today, when couples are required to wait from four to six years from the point of application, it doesn't make sense to prolong the wait any more than necessary. Therefore, we feel it is appropriate to consider adoption during the process of working through the feelings heretofore described. Presumably, by the time the placement is made, the feelings will have been resolved.

Once adoptive parents make the psychological adjustments to their unique situation, they can go on to tackle the other factors which interfere with their attempts to obtain a comfortable sense of entitlement. They still must confront the task of dealing with the societal attitude towards the institution of adoption—

attitudes which emphasize the differences between the two types of parenthood, and which convey only conditional acceptance of parenthood via adoption. This societal ambivalence is reflected in our patterns of speech and our mores. Consider one of our best known axioms: "Blood is thicker than water." Such views lead to a certain defensiveness in adoptive parents, who are expected to respond undefensively to remarks from relatives as, "Now maybe you can have one of your own." People who make such tactless remarks obviously do not realize the prejudice these remarks contain, nor their potential for hurting.

Consider, also, the terms we use in describing birth parents: "natural", "real", and "own." This may imply that adoptive parents are somehow unnatural or unreal or that parenthood by adoption is an inferior form of parenthood. Yet, these terms continue to be used, not only by lay persons, but also by professionals in the field, seemingly unaware of the biological chauvinism they are fostering.

Even some apparently positive attitudes contain seeds of doubt about the legitimacy of adoption, as the choice of words used by well intended friends continue to emphasize the differentness of this form of parenthood. Undue congratulations containing subtle messages are heaped on the couple. Remarks like, "How lucky for the child to have parents like you!" are not infrequently made. Many remarks of this nature reflect the rescue fantasy by implying that the child, perhaps the product of a union between "inadequate" people, is rescued from a life of blight and neglect. Such remarks would rarely, if ever, be made to parents following the birth of their child. In fact, one would more likely say to new (biological) parents, "How lucky you are to have such a beautiful child!"

In an interesting study of community attitudes toward adoption, Kirk (1964) found that nine out of ten couples heard such remarks as "Isn't it wonderful of you to have taken in this child!" and "This child looks so much like you that he (she) could be your own!" Four of five were asked, "Tell me, what do you know about the child's background?" One out of two parents was told: "He is a darling baby, and after all, you never know for sure how even your own will turn out." One out of three heard: "How lucky you didn't have to go through the trouble of pregnancy like I did." Finally, one out of five heard: "How well you care for the child, just like a real mother."

Adoptive parents should realize that it is not necessary to remain passive in response to such remarks. Since people do not intend for their remarks to hurt, it is reasonable and appropriate to correct these "well wishers." A question such as "what do you know of the child's parents?" should be responded with "what would you like to know about us?" Through the uncomfortable few moments that follow comes a greater appreciation of just what adoption means to the adoptive family. The same advice is suggested for the words "real," "natural," and "own." Such means of handling these seemingly innocent and tactless remarks will have the effect of a public education effort, which, in turn, will reduce the tendency of uninformed people to emit such derogatory utterances in the future.

The problem with the word "real" is that is suggests a comparison, usually of an invidious nature. Once you label parents as real (biological), you ipso facto suggest unreal or false parents (adoptive). This can directly affect adoptive parents' feelings of rightfulness to the child. This being the case, many parents feel the need to prove their fitness to the parental standard, and frequently attempt to do so in outlandish ways (e.g. buying the child everything s/he desires), leading to an overindulged child with all the attendant problems associated therewith.

On the other hand, adoption is often viewed in positive terms. People who adopt children are congratulated by relatives, friends and other well-wishers. Baby gifts are sent and the entire occasion is recognized publicly. Some parents even send announcements, modified to reflect the unique way the child came into the family. One such announcement came in the form of a legal document.

*STATE OF BLISS)	IN THE FAIRYLAND FEDERAL COURT
COUNTY OF NOD)	1986 SPRING TERM
IN RE THE MATTER OF THE BIRTH) OF JEAN LYNN JONES, INFANT)	CAUSE NO. B801

PETITION FOR ORDER FOR NOTICE OF INTERESTED PARTIES

Comes now Herbert J. Jones and Patsy A. Jones, husband and wife, Petitioners herein, and for their Petition say as follows:

---

*The writers are indebted to Melvin Daniel for the development of this "petition," the names of which are fictionalized.

1. That on January 5, 1986, at 4:30 a.m., a little girl was born.
2. That the said little girl weighed seven (7) pounds and thirteen (13) ounces at birth.
3. That the said little girl was twenty-one (21) inches long at birth.
4. That on January 6, 1986, the Cook Superior Court, Probate Division, entered an Order placing the temporary custody of said child with your Petitioners herein, namely, Herbert R. Jones and Patsy A. Jones, for the purpose of adoption of said infant.
5. That the said little girl is to be named Jean Lynn Jones.
6. That the said little girl, namely, Jean Lynn Jones, is a delight to her parents, Herbert R. Jones and Patsy A. Jones, your Petitioners herein, and her sister, Sally Jones.
7. That although said child is not of our own making, she nevertheless is miraculously our own. She may not have grown under our heart, but she is growing in it.

The child is viewed, in this case, as an integral part of his/her new family, and the parents are free to experience the joys of parenthood—joys which adoptive parents can experience as fully as other parents, provided they have resolved the conflicts previously identified and developed a sense of entitlement to their child.

CHAPTER 4

GENETIC ASPECTS OF ADOPTION

The following questions were raised by adoptive parents during a number of our parenting classes. We decided to use a question and answer format in providing information to adoptive parents. The answers were provided by Anne J. Stump, M.D., a board certified pediatrician in the Indianapolis area.

Q #1   *What kind of concerns do adoptive parents have about the health and prenatal care of the birth mother?*

A #1   As adoptive parents, we want to be sure that the birth mother has had regular prenatal visits with skilled gynecologists or family physicians and that she has had guidance in prenatal nutrition. We want to be sure that any of her chronic health problems such as diabetes, hypertension and thyroid disorders have been treated throughout the nine months. We are also concerned that any acute illnesses and venereal disease have been promptly diagnosed and treated. In general, we wish for our child to have the healthiest environment possible during its prenatal life. I have been impressed with what good prenatal care most biologic mothers obtain and how they want to "make" the healthiest baby possible for adoptive parents. It is reassuring to have talked with some of them after delivery to understand how relieved they are to have created the healthiest baby possible for an anxious set of adoptive parents.

Q #2   *How much should we be concerned about drugs, smoking and alcohol affecting the child?*

A #2   Actually, we are not sure what amount or at what stages in fetal life pot smoking causes problems. It is known that hard drugs cause problems such as growth retardation and prematurity in babies; a newborn may even go through drug withdrawal symptoms if the birth mother has been on drugs close to the time of delivery. Alcohol definitely can cause some problems, particularly during the first trimester. The Fetal Alcohol Syndrome includes varying degrees of developmental, anatomic, growth and perhaps even psychological problems ranging from mild to severe, depending on the amount of maternal alcohol ingestion. Cigarette smoking may be linked to retarded placental and fetal growth resulting in small and slightly premature babies but does not cause anatomic anomalies.

Q #3 *What condition may the biologic father also have contributed to the unborn child?*

A #3 The father's drug and smoking history probably does not contribute to the newborn nearly as much as the mother's ingestion. Studies are not conclusive how much paternal effect there is.

Q #4 *How much effect from mental and alcohol problems is passed from the second generation or birth grandparents?*

A #4 Research is indicating that alcoholism as a disease may be linked to inheritance. On the other hand, environmental influences probably far outweigh any genetic tendencies. Some psychiatric disorders may also be more genetically related than was previously thought. I don't think that a family history of a grandparent with alcoholism or mental disorder would prevent me from adopting a particular child because the environmental and psychological components are so important.

Q #5 *What kind of hereditary diseases or traits and possible birth defects should adoptive parents be made aware of before they decide to adopt a particular child? And, how much concern should be placed on a positive genetic background?*

A #5 There is a whole gamut of birth defects and syndromes, some of which are not genetically inherited. Birth defects such as congenital heart disease, missing extremities, and clubbed foot are not hereditary—they are conditions that just happen. On the other hand, hemophilia, sickle cell, cystic fibrosis, and Huntington's chorea are examples of inherited conditions which vary from dominant inheritance to recessive (only one out of four). Down's Syndrome is a chromosomal defect usually without any family history. Some conditions such as muscular dystrophy and albinism may be either inherited or caused by gene mutations and thus occur sporadically. Disease entities such as hypertension, early onset heart disease, obesity, seizures, and diabetes definitely have hereditary tendencies. Prematurity and neonatal asphyxia with complications, such as cerebral palsy, of course, are not inherited entities. In other words, some family histories should be reviewed with concern while a few very specific questions may even require genetic counseling. However, it is important for us to realize what a very small proportion of babies have defects, whether inherited or spontaneous, compared to all the normal and perfect babies born. As adoptive parents, we also need to realize that none of us has a flawless family history (we all have relatives who have died, and most of us will never live to be 100!), and it's not fair to expect our child to be perfect or come from perfect "registered" genes!

Adopting a child with average or above average intelligence and potential is probably the biggest concern of parents adopting a supposed "normal" infant or child. Unfortunately in several circumstances, I've realized that adoptive couples were more critical of the child's individual potential or I.Q. than with their own accomplishments or with a biologic child's potential.

Medically speaking, the pendulum swings between philosophies of genetically inherited versus environmental intelligence and achievement potentials. There is no absolute in percentages of genetics versus environment. Of course, most adoptive parents want to believe and probably convince themselves that environmental security, love, education, and challenge during childhood form the individual's ultimate personality and position in life far more than genetic factors.

Q #6 *How truthfully do biologic parents answer questions about their health or family history?*

A #6 I have found biological parents to be pretty honest in relaying family and medical history. In some situations this information, unfortunately, is filed by adoption agencies and is not shared with the actual adoptive parents. In other situations, particularly adoptions that utilize individual counseling, the adoptive family and the birth mother are given a very adequate exchange of information including family and medical history, intelligence potentials, and even religious and social descriptions.

Presently with such a demand for adoptive children, most birth mothers do not need to fear that their child is not acceptable for adoption, so they are truthful and open in relating family, medical, and drug histories. We need to accept that there may be a certain element of risk in not knowing everything about a child, but we trust the professionals such as social worker, physician,and attorney who are assisting us in order to make a well informed decision as to accepting this child.

Q #7 *How soon in a baby's development can you tell if a child is normal in mental and learning abilities?*

A #7 The initial neurological exam (which includes reflexes, head control, quality of cry, (etc.) can differentiate some babies with potential development problems. However, some delays may not be apparent until the child is several months or several years old, such as in some forms of cerebral palsy, motor skill delays, verbal delay, autism, and specific learning disorders. Other factors such as prenatal and neonatal growth rate, head size and growth rate, and early childhood illnesses also determine developmental potential. Apgar scores from 1 to 10 are given to the baby at 1 and 5 minutes after birth. These scores indicate the newborn's respiratory effort, heart rate, color, and muscle tone and indicate how well the baby tolerated labor, delivery, and adaptation to the outside world. The Apgar scores, however, are not indicators for long term health or development.

Q #8 *Is it possible to have a pediatrician examine the baby right away?*

A #8 Yes, it is possible; and I recommend that you arrange for a pediatrician to examine the baby shortly after birth. In private adoptions, it is often possible for the adoptive parents to even request a particular pediatrician; however, this needs to be arranged with both the lawyer and physician. I suggest that adoptive parents meet with their prospective pediatrician in a "Prenatal Conference" setting even before the birth of the child to discuss the hospital visit, newborn care, and health maintenance visits. Your pediatrician will discuss child care questions such as types of formula, bottles, baby's clothing requirements, car seat safety, types of diapers, toy stimulation, signs of illness, umbilical cord care, circumcision care and other health care necessities.

Q #9   *What about anesthetics used during delivery?*

A #9   The medical trend is away from general anesthetic for delivery and more toward epidural or local anesthetic. Many birth mothers desire to be awake during delivery. The majority of deliveries via general anesthetic are now done for fetal or maternal distress such as in an emergency C-section.

Q #10 *How do parents select a pediatrician?*

A #10 A good way to select a pediatrician is to inquire from friends and relatives in your area who they might recommend. From personal experience, many adoptive parents desire a pediatrician who has previously cared for adoptive parents' children and who understands some of the special concerns and circumstances that adoptive families encounter. A physician that you can talk with and that you trust is extremely important.

Q #11 *One question the lawyer or agency will probably ask is, "Do you desire circumcision if it's a boy?" If it's a girl, obviously you don't have to worry about it. What's new on the horizon about circumcision?*

A #11 Circumcision was originally a religious tradition. In the U.S., circumcision then became a cleanliness, maintenance, and even a tumor prevention measure. From there it became almost an automatic procedure on male infants. In recent years, however, the pendulum has swung away from circumcisions. Now the American Academy of Pediatrics suggests that circumcision is a religious or cosmetic and not a medically indicated procedure. Most physicians have their personal preference, but feel that circumcision is a parental decision. Particularly with adopted infants, the procedure may be done as an outpatient, or even in the physician's office if it has not been done before the baby has been released from the hospital.

But in all fairness, I must add that there is another part of this question that must be addressed, apart from the purely medical consideration. This has to do with the male child's psychological development. Boys do like to look like their fathers, and so if the father is circumcised but the boy is not, he may wonder why he has this extra layer of foreskin. At that point, and I'm probably talking about a 4 or 5 year old, circumcision is undoubtedly a traumatic event whereas in an infant, it is not. So despite the Academy's recommendations advising against circumcision as a medical "luxury," (and I have no quarrel with their position), the actual decision must be made by the family, taking into account this family perspective.

Q #12 *Have you had the experience of adoptive parents bringing their child to you and the nurse asks all about the child's history, then after you review the history data, the mother then whispers, "Oh, he's ADOPTED," or "that's not pertinent?"*

A #12 Unfortunately this encounter has probably occurred in most physicians' offices. However, not all the blame should go on the nurse or physician. Most nurses do not routinely ask, "Is your child biologic or adopted?". Some offices or clinics may care for only a few adopted children, while other offices may provide health care for many adoptive families and be more in tune with family health histories, growth patterns, and charting that neither hides nor exposes the child's adoption. It is the parents' responsibility to honestly acknowledge and remind health care providers at the proper time and in the proper manner that their child's health does not have their biologic tendencies or heredity.

Q #13 *Should parents tell the school and teachers that their child is adopted?*

A #13 Most school situations have no bearing on whether or not a child is biologically related to his parents. In some special situations such as learning disability, gifted abilities or more often, an extreme behavior problem, it may be beneficial for the teacher to know that the child is adopted. Otherwise, some school personnel may not know how to use the information. As well adjusted adoptive parents, we should neither disguise nor advertise our child's adoption. Personnel may not know how to use the information.

Q #14 *Do you have a philosophy of adoptive parenthood?*

A #14 The majority of adoptive parents desire the opportunity to share their lives with a healthy, normal child and rear the youngster through childhood and adolescence to adulthood. Most of these parents have experienced infertility workups or longterm health problems. Generally the adoptive parents are not overly critical of the family medical history or genes of the child, but desire a "normal" child. However, "normal" denotes a wide range in health, anatomic development, intelligence, psychologic adjustment, and environment.

The lawyers, psychologists, social workers, and physicians that are involved with the personal aspects of each adoption are attempting to create compatible parent-child combinations and families. They realize that high risk children with special health and genetic problems require special parents.

In summary, adoptive parents must remember that parenting is a privilege and opportunity that they have chosen to share their lives, love, and resources with a dependent younger human being. And what a blessing it is!!

CHAPTER 5

THE LEGAL PROCESS IN ADOPTION: INDEPENDENT PLACEMENT ALTERNATIVE

A long standing controversy in adoption practice revolves around the persons involved in the adoption. Most (non-relative) adoptions are handled by licensed child-placing agencies. However, with a decrease in the number of healthy infants available for adoption through agencies, there has been a corresponding increase in the placement of adoptions through an intermediary —usually an attorney and/or physician. This is sometimes referred to as "gray market," distinguishing it from "black market," which is illegal. Such non-agency placements are permitted in all states except Connecticut, Massachusetts, Minnesota, Delaware and Michigan.

There are many arguments for and against private placements but research studies have revealed very few differences, either short term or long term, between agency and independent placements. This was the major finding of a fairly recent study carried out by the Child Welfare League of America (CWLA), the national, standard-setting agency in child welfare, which offered the following recommendations in regard to adoptive placements (Meezan, Katz & Russo, 1978):*

1. A requirement of preplacement investigations of prospective adoptive homes (already in effect in seven states), with agencies given ample time to do a thorough job in evaluating a given home, based on the same standards currently applied in agency adoptions. This would help to guarantee a suitable home to

---

*A series of nine recommendations are made. Our comments to some of these points are interspersed and will be self-evident to the reader.

a child, and negate the tendency of judges to allow children to remain in homes that may not meet their needs. This way no bonds would be formed between adoptive parents and child prior to approval of the home.

2. Mandatory involvement during the preplacement investigation of all parties to the adoption, so that they are aware of their rights and alternatives open to them. Such involvement would allow qualified personnel to offer counseling to the biological mothers who want it, and prepare the adoptive couple for the task of rearing a child they would eventually adopt. It would also guarantee the rights of the biological father and ensure proper termination of these rights. Such mandated involvement would also expedite resolution in the event that the child is born with a physical or developmental disability, or is unacceptable to an adoptive couple for some other reason.

3. Prior to or immediately after placement (and following voluntary relinquishment), a judicial proceeding terminating parental rights, so that the right of the adoptive parents to security in their relationship with the child is guaranteed. The consent for relinquishing parental rights cannot be purchased with cash or any other thing of value, and must be a free and voluntary act in order to constitute a valid, binding, and enforceable contract.

It is our position that to argue either for or against independent placement is a fruitless venture. Anyone can cite a case of improper handling of an adoption (by either an attorney or agency worker), which does not justify the elimination of that mode of practice by those who are carrying out their professional responsibilities in a disciplined and ethical manner. What is really at stake here is the outlining of a set of procedures that stand the test of sound ethical practice.

In accordance with this norm, it is essential that the biological mother be presented with the options available to her so that she is not coerced into any decision based upon false or inadequate information. In brief, the "informed consent"* must not be violated. She must be free to make a decision about her baby *without* such guilt-inducing statements as "giving up

---

*This is a legal term meaning, in this case, that she fully understands the permanency and irrevocability of her signed consent.

the baby is the charitable thing to do, the humane thing to do — as you'll be able to have another baby sometime in the future and these people (the prospective adoptive parents) won't." Furthermore, she must be presented with information regarding public welfare and other financial assistance programs relative to medical care, hospital expenses, and caring for herself and the baby. (How the counseling process is carried out is dealt with in greater detail in Chapter 10.)

Meeting the CWLA's recommendation necessitates following proper procedures for the termination or relinquishment of the biological parent's rights. Differentiation must be made, however, between these two parent figures. If the parents are unmarried, the birth father has historically been given little recognition in the legal process. The Supreme Court of the United States does, however, dictate that parental rights may not be terminated without notification of the birth father regarding the impending adoption. This decision grew out of a precedent-setting case in 1972, *Stanley* vs. *Illinois*. Mr. Stanley and his common law wife had several children. Illinois had a statute which held that the children of unwed fathers become wards of the state in the event of the mother's death, without any notice of such proceeding being given to the putative father. The mother died and, accordingly, the Cook County Department of Public Welfare in Chicago took the children and placed them in foster homes without any notification to Mr. Stanley. Mr. Stanley sued the State of Illinois, holding that the statute was unconstitutional on the grounds that it violated the Fourteenth Amendment due process and protection clauses. His argument was that he was dealt with differently than other parents, all of whom would have been provided a hearing on their fitness before their children are removed from their custody. The case went to the United States Supreme Court, which decided, in effect, that regardless of status, the birth father was entitled to notice that foster or adoptive placement of his children was pending. Mr. Stanley was then granted a hearing. It was determined, however, that placement with him was not in the children's best interests and the children were removed permanently from his care. The result of this Supreme Court action, however, had far-reaching overtones. All of the state legislatures, fearing similar cases, passed statutes or checked their laws carefully to see that they required notification of the birth father, entitling him to a hearing.

The court decisions have divided the birth father's circumstances into two categories. The first situation involves what the court believes to be a casual relationship. The second situation is one in which there is greater permanency of the man-woman relationship, such as living together over a period of time. In the former situation, the birth father is entitled to only minor consideration, but in the latter situation, his claims to the child are elevated substantially.

4. The legal requirement that an adoption petition be filed no later than one (1) year after the placement of the child. This would guarantee that a determination on the status of the child would be made expeditiously and that the child would not remain in legal "limbo."

5. The protection of the anonymity of the adoptive couples and biological parents until the child has reached his/her majority should be guaranteed to eliminate the possibility of blackmail and harassment of one party by the other. Such protection might be waived, if both parties were agreeable. In addition, any statutes requiring the revealing of the identity of the biological adoptive parents to each other, or requiring a meeting between these parties, should be eliminated.

6. There should be established by law, and/or by the professional associations of the various intermediaries, reasonable fee ranges for intermediaries in the adoption process. Such established ranges would, it is hoped, reduce the willingness of the various parties to charge or pay fees above those that are "reasonable and customary."

7. An itemized declaration of all costs in the adoption at the time of filing an adoption petition should be a requirement so that the laws regarding the buying and selling of children could be more strictly monitored. In addition, a list of legally reimbursable expenses should be established so that biological mothers would not be induced to relinquish their children for monetary or other gains.

8. The establishment or strengthening of statutes concerning the sale of children, with mandatory prosecution of suspected abusers is critical in order to deter any trafficking of "black market" babies. Related to this should be the establishment

or strengthening of penalty provisions in the law so that abusers face heavy, rather than nominal, penalties. In addition, all parties to the adoption should be held liable for action in the adoption. Not only should the facilitator be prosecuted for arranging adoptions for exorbitant fees, but adoptive couples willing to pay fees above the established rates, and biological parents accepting payments except for medical and hospital expenses should also be held accountable for their actions.

9. State laws should be passed which prohibit the importation of children from or exportation of children to another state for the purpose of placement or adoption in an unrelated home except by a licensed social agency. Much of the legally questionable activity appears to occur in the interstate transport of children.

These nine recommendations are self-explanatory and their intent is clear. Anyone handling a private placement should review those points. The conclusion of the adoption study conducted by the CWLA was that private placement is to be viewed as a viable option to agency placement, but only with consideration of these aforementioned points.

There are a number of other legal and procedural issues of consideration in the adoption process. Many of these concerns and responsibilities are relevant to both private placement adoptions and those handled by an adoption agency. While the principles and procedures involved in sound professional placement practice extends to both agency and private placements, we believe that prospective adoptive families and professionals dealing with these families in a private placement would benefit from being aware of the issues and procedures awaiting them.

The initial interview with the biological mother is extremely important. A thorough medical history must be obtained which should include information on any health problems or conditions, hereditary diseases, prenatal care, and the mother's use of drugs or alcohol. The interview should also yield information regarding the mother's interests, accomplishments, school records, extra curricular activities, special idiosyncratic talents (e.g., music or photographic memory), goals and aspirations, and family social history. This information is needed in order to provide to the adopting family a "picture" of the biological mother, and so that the information can be available to the child when he or she becomes curious later on in life. The placement worker should independently verify as much of the information as possible, as parental anxieties seem to lessen somewhat with the knowledge that a thorough job is being done.

A family counselor should be made available to the birth mother, as the process of surrendering a child for adoption is difficult. In private adoptions, the attorney should make clear to the biological mother that he is representing the adoptive parents. Even in obtaining counseling for the biological mother, the intermediary is acting in the client-parent's interests. While obtaining that service allows the biological mother to get help in healing some emotional scars, it also helps insure that whatever consents are ultimately gained and signed by the mother are going to be judged more objectively by virtue of it being executed after independent counselling.

Handling of the consents, as stated earlier, is critically important. The consent forms should be carefully explained to the biological mother, reviewed again at a later stage of pregnancy, and reviewed a third time in the hospital after the baby is born. In this way, the attorney or intermediary is assured that the biological mother understands what she is reading and understands the nature of the process. Another essential precaution in guaranteeing the validity of the consents is to make sure that at the initial meeting with the biological mother that all alternatives available to the biological parents are discussed. She must be made aware of the various services offered by private and public agencies, prenatal and medical care assistance programs available to her, and her right to her own attorney, if so desired.

The intermediary must discuss with the biological and adoptive parents the coverage of costs, the payment of medical bills and the payment of hospital bills. Such discussion should address the possibilities of complications during the delivery, procedures and responsibilities if the baby would have serious medical problems, and the consequences if either party changes their mind about the adoption. The intermediary must discuss these possibilities and bind all parties to the understanding and agreement.

The birth mother should be informed about her assurance of privacy. At the present time, most states have records which are closed and, unless there is "good cause" shown, she can complete this painful event without fear of repercussions in her future life from past events. Although the law may change at some point, under present policies in most states, there is no chance in a conventional form of adoption of the adoptive parents obtaining her name or address, and vice versa. As previously stated, however, such precautions are violated in an "open adoption" practice.

It is advisable to send the consent forms to the birth mother prior to the baby's birth, even though they can not be signed until the birth. It is best for her to have had the forms for a period of time, and to have obtained full prior explanation of the forms and responsibilities between the parties in the adoption. These procedures are helpful in that they provide evidence that the birth mother understood her actions and the procedures involved clearly. Such preparation helps protect the adoptive parents against the possibility that the birth mother may later change her mind and want the baby returned to her. It also removes some of the pressures and insecurities for the birth mother by helping her know what to expect and prepare herself emotionally for the anticipatory sense of loss. The birth mother also needs to sign a consent form for examination of the child in the hospital, as well as a waiver of the physician-patient privilege. This should be done prior to the time the baby is born. The adoptive parents should have their physician examine the baby in the hospital and perform the circumcision, if that is desired. A consent to examine the child needs to be prepared and signed in order for the physician to be allowed to examine the child. The medical waiver must be prepared and signed so that additional biological medical history can be obtained. This consent is forwarded along with a letter to the hospital and its social service department in order to effect a smooth transition without problems in the hospital regarding the delineation of responsibility.

The hospital social worker plays a key role in this process. S/he should be contacted prior to registration to obtain for the biological mother a private room so that the biological mother is not presented with the problems and conflicts of being in a maternity ward with mothers who are nursing their babies. Sometimes the mother can be placed in a gynecological ward as opposed to an obstetrical ward. This reduces some of the trauma in the proceedings. The social worker should be made aware of the legal and psychological counseling the mother has received, and the social worker should be informed as to the handling of the consents. Often the consents are signed with a hospital social worker present. Within two weeks after leaving the hospital, the biological mother should have seen the welfare department or appropriate agency. With procedures handled thusly, all parties should be confident that the biological mother was completely informed of her rights and she would not be able to later persuade a judge that she didn't understand what she was doing. This crisp, clear and straightforward process also gives a sense of professionalism and finality to the process. No signals can be misread by the birth mother which can give her any inkling that this is not a full termination of her rights.

The adoptive parents are entitled to have all the medical information on the child. They should also obtain adoption-specific family counseling. Inasmuch as there are many societal biases toward adopted children, counseling sensitizes them to the issues and helps them cope with such biases. It also allows the counselor to prepare a report on them which can be presented in their behalf at the initial filing for adoption. A report from a qualified social worker* can help an attorney demonstrate to the court that the parents are sensitized to the adoption process, that the marriage is stable, and that it is a good home for placement. Additionally, the intermediary must go over financial responsibilities with the adoptive parents. There is also a risk with private placement that if the baby dies or if the baby is not medically adoptable, the adoptive parents may have to assume the responsibility for several days of hospital care.

Most insurance programs of adoptive parents will provide for coverage for the child from the date of birth or after the initial order for custody if signed by the court. Adoptive parents should examine their insurance coverage and the financial department of the hospital should be informed regarding the insurance coverage on the child. That is very important, especially if there is a premature birth or complications where the baby is otherwise fine and medically adoptable, because coverage usually can be initiated from birth. Further, there are certain responsibilities the attorney has to the court: 1) the duty to disclose the reasonableness of attorney's fees; 2) the duty to disclose the reasonableness of the medical bills and the amount of the hospital bills; 3) the duty to report to the court of any irregularities in charges. It is this author's (F.I.M.) personal opinion that any law should

---

*Ideally, a person with a Master of Social Work degree from an accredited School of Social Work.

include the requirement of an affidavit of financial disclosure, similar to Bankruptcy Law procedure. The attorney or agency should submit an affidavit to the court as to how much the fees are, what services were rendered, how much was taken into the trust account and dispersed to the hospital or the doctor. The court could then feel very comfortable with the placement. Agencies should also be required to filing of such an affidavit. Such comparable procedures would provide all the necessary safeguards to the child entering into his new family home under the highest of ethical standards.

CHAPTER 6

THE TELLING PROCESS

Without a doubt, the telling of adoption to a child is the most unique, but at the same time, most troublesome aspect of adoption. Many parents view this process with trepidation as the differences between adoptive and biological parenthood come to the fore, whereas previously any differences could be discounted or even denied.

It may be well to examine the nature of such anticipated problems. As identified in our previous work, the telling brings to the child's mind another, and perhaps, competitive (depending on the couple's handling of entitlement issues) set of parents. That is to say, the very act of telling brings birth parents into the family system ("they are also part of you") and *may*, therefore, jeopardize the exclusiveness of the parent-child relationship. If the adoptive parents are still struggling to develop feelings of entitlement and are uncomfortable with telling the child about an original set of parents, the child may well respond more to the parents' anxiety than to the content which is meant to be conveyed. Finally, through the telling, the parents are faced with the need to explain why they needed to resort to adoption in the first place. To the extent that the telling stirs up angry or resentful feelings because of unresolved feelings related to infertility or sexual adequacy, the spontaneity and warmth recommended in the telling may be severely compromised.

It is our view that parents need suggestions on various ways in which to tell their child of the adoption; we do not think that they should be led to believe that there is only one right way to tell. In the adoptive parent classes which we offer, between 80 and 90 percent of the couples pose this concern as the primary motivating factor for taking the course. It is also our view that parents are often needlessly anxious and concerned about the child's reaction and ability to handle the "news". Such anxiety may reflect the parents' projection of their own discomfort and lack of coping skills. If the parents have worked through their feelings about whose child this really is, the "homework," in a sense, has been done.

When the child asks, "Where did I come from?", it is important to answer his question openly and without hesitation. We view the telling as a very important time in the child's life span and development—a special moment, if you will, between the parents and the child. We liken the importance of this special moment to a proposal of marriage, or the actual marriage rite, in which two people committed themselves to a lifelong bond. It is conceptualized as happy moment—one that will always be remembered with positive feelings. The telling can be a most gratifying experience—one which adds to, rather than detracts from, a feeling of belonging and identity. Instead of perceiving the occasion as a threat to the parent-child relationship, parents should view it as a challenge and as a way of solidifying a positive bond. Research findings confirm this view: The more open the subject of adoption, the better the child's adjustment to it. (Witmer, 1963)

There is one basic principle which we believe all adoptive parents should understand and adhere to: the ease with which the child fully accepts his adoptedness is directly related to the degree of the adoptive parents' success in accepting (and feeling entitled to) their own status as adoptive parents. There are a number of clues which might be interpreted as signals of the degree of such acceptance. If the parents can discuss the fact of adoption openly, without fear, guilt, or embarrassment, rather than either avoiding the topic of feeling the need to reveal it with every conceivable opportunity, the indications are that acceptance has taken place. If, on the other hand, they are struggling with fantasies of how their own biological children might have looked and behaved, or are reacting emotionally or defensively to the news of a friend's pregnancy or birth of a friend's child, this indicates that underlying attitudes need to be more fully explored. Under such circumstances, discussions about adoption may take place at inappropriate times and convey to the child a sense that something is wrong. *Either too much talking about adoption or not talking about it at all indicates that there are problems in acceptance.* Parents should also realize that children respond more readily to feelings and nuances than they do to what is being said (Smith and Miroff, 1981).

The issue of telling children about their adoptive status is controversial as to how and when to best tell a child, and there is disagreement among professionals as to the effects of the telling process on the children. We feel it necessary to stress a point which has the full backing of our clinical experience and is compatible with the case studies cited. It is simply this: When adoption is poorly handled in a family, it not the fact of adoption that makes for emotional disturbance, but something more basic. It has to do with the nature of relationships with a family, and whether people are open with each other and caring about each other's needs. It has to do with the openness or closeness of communication and whether it is honest, trustworthy or, on the other hand, rigid and dishonest. It has to do with loving and caring feelings, or perhaps a perception of loving and caring feelings, or the obverse, cold and high critical. It has to do with how a family communicates together. It is, simply put, the general dysfunction in a family that makes for the disturbance in a(n) (adopted) child, not the fact of his/her adoptedness.

Consider the following case. Mr. and Mrs. R. were an older couple who had adopted Keith when he was four days old. Mr. R. had a very successful career as a building contractor and Mrs. R. was a "retired" teacher. The placement was effected when the R's were 49 and 48, respectively, considerably older than the norm. The R's had already adopted one child, William, when the caseworker showed up at the house unannounced, holding a scrawny, obviously sickly child, and asked whether they would keep the child for a matter of weeks until an adoptive placement could be made. The R's accepted the challenge and did not think that this would pose a problem for their eight month old William. Keith was never removed from the home but subsequently adopted by the R's. In time, the R's adopted a third boy although this placement was by design, not happenstance.

Over the years, Keith began to exhibit serious behavior problems. Although of normal intelligence, he failed all of his school courses, and engaged in lying, stealing, and fighting. He did not feel close to either parent and frequently felt scapegoated by his two brothers. (The parents invariably took the other boy's side in a sibling dispute.) It was clear that every member in the family lined up against Keith and told him that he was "the weird one, the oddball, the one with the problem." By the time Mrs. R. brought Keith in for therapy, the hostility and sense of alienation had become irreversible. There was one particular message that Keith repeatedly referred to in their encounters. It was that whenever a conflict situation occurred between Mrs. R. and Keith, and she was clearly disappointed in him, she asked (him) if that was the treatment she deserved for taking him in and, in effect, rescuing him. Keith expressed how angry these remarks made him.

Again, it is not the fact of adoption that makes for the good or poor adjustment, but how it is handled within the family. Had Mrs. R. not handled conflict situations by resurrecting the adoption issue, it is likely that the problems might not have been as severe as they were.

Social agencies tend to take a position of openness about adoption from the very beginning of a child's life. It is common practice to instruct parents to begin to tell the child of his adoption as early as possible in his development and certainly before he enters school. The child is to be told of his chosenness to diminish any tendency for the child to think of himself as not having been wanted (by the birth parents). This practice not only eliminates a potentially traumatic experience for the child who suddenly learns of his adoption through the careless and insensitive remarks of friends and relatives, but also provides the child with the opportunity of integrating the "adopted" self-image into his thinking from the beginning.

It is clear, however, that some parents do not handle the situation well. In situations where the telling process stirs up unresolved feelings, the resulting anxiety is usually manifested in one of two ways. The first way is exemplified by the parent who may go to great lengths to avoid the subject matter altogether. On the other hand, if adoption is discussed repeatedly, to the point of "overkill," this is also a warning signal that something has gone awry in the telling of the child's adoption. The effect of this on the child may be to threaten his identification with, and integration into, the adoptive family. These polar positions of too little or too much telling reflect an inability to deal with adoption.

Actually, the whole idea of telling has come under scrutiny in recent years. One critic questions its wisdom on the grounds that the knowledge of different birth origins is too painful for a child and that he is better off spared such information (Ansfield, 1970). He argues that the child need not deal with such an emotionally charged issue as the reality of two sets of parents, nor bear the impact of original rejection. Other critics suggest that while the adoptee has the right to know about the fact of his birth, the telling should be delayed until he is of school age and has already passed through the most formative years of his life (Peller, 1961). This argument, it seems to us, assumes that the growing child will not ask questions about where he came from until he is, say, nine or ten years old.

There are a number of admonitions from various authors in reference to the telling. Schecter (1960) points out that parents, attempting to be forthright and natural about the subject, may repeatedly focus on the child's adoptive status (e.g., "how is my adopted child today?") in their conversations with each other, and thereby communicate their anxiety to the child. Repetition of the adoption story and how "we picked you" may come to connote something "bad" about being adopted, thus increasing the child's anxiety about it. Browning (1942) takes an even more pessimistic view of adoption as an interfering variable in the child's course of normal development when she refers to the intrapsychic effects of learning that one is an adopted child. Her view is that once a child has been told of his adoption, he invariably must cope with the feeling of having been deserted by his "real" parents, that he does not "belong," and that he is different from other children. She concludes that, in spite of parents' total acceptance of the child, this inevitable interpretation of his adoptive status must profoundly affect his self-concept and leave him feeling inferior and not a real part of any family group.

We do admit that there is some validity to some of these theoretical positions. The argument of delayed telling makes a good deal of sense, in some respects. When a child is struggling with working through his feelings toward his parents, to introduce him to a fantasied set of parents may sow some seeds of confusion. Later on in life he may indeed be more psychologically prepared to deal with the idea of two sets of parents.

Despite the plausibility of these arguments, the fact of the matter is that there are grave risks associated with either of these approaches (no telling and delayed telling). While they may make some sense theoretically, they offer little in the way of practical solutions for adoptive parents. If a three year old comes to his mother and asks if he grew in her tummy, either she says "yes" or "no." If she answers in the affirmative, she has lied to him; if she answers in the negative, then she is already discussing adoption with him. The reader should bear in mind that these theoretical positions are not derived from a sample of "normal" adoptees, but from clinical impressions of a sample of emotionally disturbed children who have, coincidentally, been adopted. More will be said about this in our chapter on "Research Findings." For the time being, let us only comment that it is the gravest of methodological errors to generalize the findings of a clinical sample to a non-clinical one. This is essentially what these critics have done in their criticism of early telling.

There are other reasons why we maintain that our position on openness in telling the young child about the adoption is a valid one. First, the no telling and delayed telling approaches falsify a relationship which is supposed to be based on openness and honesty. Honesty is a crucial element in a healthy parent-child relationship. Without honesty, there can be no relationship. Adopted children who do not learn of their adoption until late adolescence or early adulthood invariably experience feelings of betrayal and profound hurt. Ultimately, this child may come to believe that if something as fundamental and basic as a relationship between parent and child is based on a lie, then all else is a lie as well. Second, the very act of withholding the information suggests to the child that there is something wrong with adoption. The child may well think, "If my own parents can't talk about my adoption, there must be something wrong with me." Third, there is always the possibility that, since adoption is invariably a matter of public knowledge to relatives and friends, the child will hear of it first from another source. Fourth, the child is entitled to know the truth about his origins. The question, therefore, involves an ethical consideration.

When, then, should a child be told of his adoption? There is no universally correct answer. Timing depends on the readiness of the individual child. Children differ in their maturational and intellectual development, and some children are ready sooner than others. Generally, by the age of three or four, a child should have heard the word "adoption" and should have some idea of how he came to live with his parents. As stated previously, we suggest drawing a picture of the home, the hospital and the agency or attorney's office, so that the child can visualize the interrelated aspects of his "coming home." For the young child, mere words are not enough. The pictorial presentation may give him a clearer understanding of how he and his parents came together. This gives the child a visual picture of how the matching process works. For an older child, it works even better because you can include a foster home (or a series of foster homes, if that is the case). The important thing to emphasize is that he or she will be moving no more, as this adoptive home is his permanent home and family.

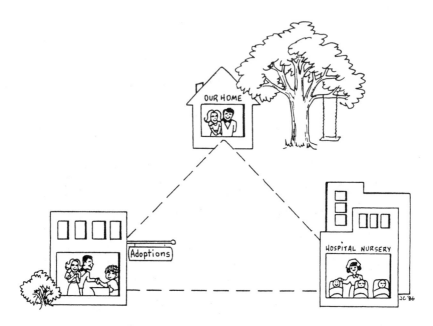

Parents should realize that a child's understanding of adoption proceeds from the simple to the more complex. The three questions he will need answers to as he grows older is (1) *What* is adoption?; (2) *How* does it happen? (i.e., the process); and (3) *Why* did it happen? The "what" and the "how" questions take a long time to understand. Up to now, we have stressed ways to convey this knowledge in an acceptable way. When the child is a little older, perhaps four or five, he may ask questions again. Although there is no one right formula for words to use in the telling, the following dialogue suggests some of the more typical questions posed by children, along with possible answers.

Child: Mommy, where did I come from?

Mother: What do you mean, honey?

Child: Johnny says he came from his mommy's tummy. Did I come from your tummy?

Mother: No, you didn't.

Child: Well, where did I come from, then?

Mother: Good question. Do you remember us using the word "adoption?"

Child: Yes.

Mother: What do you remember it means?

Child: You said it means you wanted me because you and Daddy couldn't have a baby.

Mother: Right, which also means that you came out of another woman's tummy. She was not able to care for you, so she asked that another family be picked out to love you and give you the care she was unable to give you but wanted you to have.

Child: You mean that you're not my real mommy?

Mother: Is that how you feel, that I'm not your real mommy?

Child: No, I think you are—but I'm confused.

Mother: I know it is confusing, but in time you will understand it better, I am sure. The questions you are asking are asked by every adopted child. They are normal questions. While it's a different way of coming to us that the usual way, I want you to know it's the only difference. You're our child just the same as Johnny is his mother's child and I love you and want you the same as if you had come out of my own tummy. Your daddy and I are very glad we have you and that you are one of us.

Child: Okay, Mommy. I'd like to go out and play now, okay?

It is worth examining this dialogue. First, mother does not answer the child's question until she understands exactly what he has in mind. Second, she helps him make connections between what was told on previous occasions and what she is about to

disclose. Third, she feels reasonably comfortable in revealing his origins to him, and he can accept the reality, because she accepts it. Finally, the child is allowed to express his feelings about what he has been told and about what adoption means to him. The child responds in kind to the mother's warmth and openness in discussing a matter of great importance to him. The "sugarcoating" that frequently goes along with the telling, such as "we chose you" and "you are the chosen child" is omitted.

There are those who feel that the "chosen child" concept places an inordinately difficult burden on the child to live up to great expectations. The child might well ask "chosen" for what? Others feel that it is essentially false. One adoptee told us that it was not he who was chosen; it was his parents who were chosen for him—inasmuch as the supply side of the adoptive equation was clearly in his favor. There is also some agreement on the inappropriateness of the use of the word "chosen" in a family situation which had both adopted and biological children. If the adopted child is chosen, what of the biological child? In attempting to arrive at some commonality between these two types of births, the word "wanted" seems to be much more preferable.

The importance of open communication within a family system cannot be overstated. If children are experiencing mixed feelings about being adopted or, worse yet, negative feelings, it is important to allow them to state this fact as long as the child isn't using it as a weapon for a larger allowance, a chance to stay overnight at a friend's house, or a host of other bargain-related maneuvers. Children need help in expressing their feelings and knowing that their parents care about them. If a child wants to discuss his feelings about adoption and the parents suggest that the subject matter can wait, the child may interpret this as a personal rejection. The hurt that comes with such a rebuff in a matter that is so personal with him will leave an everlasting impression. He may well have emerged from that very important encounter feeling that there was something wrong with his question or, worse, that there was something wrong with him. Instead, the mother in our dialogue revealed the truth to the child while reassuring him of her love for him and of his place in the family.

It has proved positive in our experience to refer to the birth mother as "the woman who gave birth" rather than the "mother." Particularly for children under the age of five, the idea of two mothers may be confusing. The child at this stage is ill-equipped to handle such confusion, so we suggest that the terms "mother" and "father" be reserved for those who have accepted the parenting and nurturing role. Once the child reaches adolescence, we have no objection to referring to the birth mother as "birth mother."

As indicated previously, parents should also be cautioned against overdoing the telling process. While avoidance of the subject matter may carry confusing and unhealthy messages to the child, overemphasis is also undesirable. The child wants to know about the adoption, but he does not want the fact reiterated at every opportunity. In McWhinnie's Studies of Adult Adoptees, (1967), she noted:

> None of these adopted children wanted their adoptive status shrouded in complete secrecy . . . Equally, they did not want constant reference to it. They wanted something in between, where their adopted status was acknowledged without embarrassment and then overtly forgotten so that they were treated exactly as if they were biological sons and daughters of the adopted parents . . . Thus, they were emphatic that they did

not want to be introduced as an "adopted son" or an "adopted daughter" . . . They wanted to feel they belonged in the family and were completely accepted there as a son or a daughter (p. 249).

In summary, telling the child of his adoptive status is regarded as the single important task in the (adopted) child's psychological development. While there is some disagreement in the field about the timing of the telling, the research findings repeatedly show that delayed telling is associated with heightened negative reactions on the part of the child (Witmer, 1963; Triseliotis, 1973). Parents may need some help in the technical aspects of the message, but if their feelings for the child are feelings of love and warmth, the particular words used are of little consequence. The ease with which the child accepts the news of his adoptive status is very directly related to the comfort level of the parents in accepting their own status as adoptive parents.

CHAPTER 7

PSYCHOLOGICAL DEVELOPMENT OF THE LATENCY-AGED CHILD

The latency-aged child is one who falls within the age category of seven to eleven (just prior to adolescence). The term "latency" derives from the observation that psychologically, the youngster's development is in a state of dormancy—in effect, a lull before the storm (of adolescence).

Most adoptive parents are no different than biological parents in their concern over their child's psychological development. Questions surface in the parents' minds about the best way to teach children responsibility within a value framework that stresses concern for his/her fellow human beings while striving to be competitive and successful. Adoptive parents share all of the concerns of their biological counterparts (in many cases, parents are both adoptive and biological parents), but adoptive parents have additional concerns related to the fact of adoption.

Some of these concerns (as related to adoption) fall in the medical realm, particularly if the medical history is not complete or is vague (not being sure who the birth father is, for example, or not knowing that much about him). Some of these concerns fall in the realm of uncertainty of the child's intellectual endowment. These concerns become intensified whenever there are gaps in the medical and personal history and become attenuated when such a history is reasonably complete. And, of course, if the parents have unresolved feelings and fears about their own right to the child, the situation is ripe for the projection of blame to the adoptive situation. Whatever the case, it is hard to evaluate the child's adjustment to life without taking into account the nature of the parents' adjustment in many areas of their own lives.

For the child who is adopted, this is a most critical stage. It is during this time that he comes to understand that in order for his adoption to have taken place, somebody who birthed him had to have given him up. The perception of rejection comes as an affront to a child who heretofore had thought of himself as wanted, chosen and special. It is a concern of all adoptive parents and should be dealt with forthrightly.

The literature on the child's psychological development is replete with reference to the excess psychological baggage of coming to terms with the idea that one's own parents are not the same ones who birthed him. Many authors (Peller, 1961; Schechter, 1969; Toussieng, 1962) question the reasonableness of the expectation of telling a child the story of his adoption without providing unintentionally the fantasy of rejection and desertion. Peller relates a resultant fantasy of having been kidnapped, creating "a longing for the human being from whom he has been forcibly separated" (1961). Yet at the same time, there is reference in the literature to provide the reader with a less pessimistic viewpoint. A statement by Dr. Viola Bernard typifies this position (1953):

> Since the child turns to the unknown fantasied parents, facilitated by the reality of adoption in reaction to feeling angry and hurt by his real-life adoptive parents...the most potent antidote to excessive and persistent psychological recourse to this escapist fantasy is a healthy, sincere, satisfying relationship between the child and his adoptive parents...as defined by cumulative experience of living together as a family. In emotionally healthy adoption - which includes a normal degree of mutual frustration, anxiety and hostility - the child's involvement with biological parents remains within bounds (p. 207).

There is an obvious reference to the "family romance" in this statement, a concept to be explained later in this chapter. Another psychiatrist, Irene Josselyn, offers a view centering on the nature of the parent-child relationship and the identification between the parent and child as the significant variable in the equation. She states (1956):

> ...a successful relationship between mother and child, whether an adoptive or natural mother, results in a constructive identification because of the meaningfulness that the parent has for the child. If the identification is with someone else, a true parent-child relationship does not exist (p. 16).

Obviously, one can either overplay or underplay the importance of the adoptive situation in identifying the behavioral characteristics of a particular child. While we feel it is dangerous to attribute all maladjustment to the adoptive status, it would be just as wrong to assume that the child has no feelings about it, and therefore, to be discounted. It is a variable to be considered as part and parcel of the family constellation and how the family deals with adoption is most critical. Consider the following case:

> Doug was a 12 year old who appeared at the clinic looking quite anxious. He was brought in by his parents for being disobedient at home. He sported a bruise on his face which he claimed was inflicted by his father as he was kicked downstairs. Doug went on to say that this was his own fault as he had made father angry much of the time. In fact, he stated, "I'm used to it." He stated that his father is always "on his case" for something, particularly his grades, and has told him from time to time that he will never go far in life. Doug said that his mother yells at him a lot and predicts that he will always be in trouble and be a source of embarrassment to the family.

> Regarding background information, he stated that he is one of five adoptive children but denied that any of his problems have anything to do with that. His main difficulty was in his attitude toward his father, who treats him unkindly. Regarding his parents, he feels he owes them a great deal but is bothered by the continued bickering between his parents. He looked quite sad as he told the therapist, "I have never seen them even touch each other."

This particular case is illustrative of a number of family situations in which the adoption theme might become scapegoated. Family tension was high and the family's adjustment was barely marginally adequate. Love was not fostered either between the parents or between the parents and children. Doug received very few messages from his parents that would enable him to develop a positive self-image; consequently, he engaged in a host of self-deprecatory remarks whose behavior was consistent with the theme that he would always be in trouble. Yet it was not the adoption that brought this family in for treatment although one could question what was the agency worker thinking about in placing so many children with such a psychologically impoverished set of parent figures.

In a family in which love abounds and the parents feel good about themselves as competent human beings, the child ought to receive positive strokes or reinforcements. This will help him as he attempts to integrate the idea of being adopted into the fabric of his personality. But if he is rejected by his parents, for whatever reason, this can be devastating. So how well the child deals with the adoption is in direct proportion to how the parents deal with it and the quality of the parent-child relationship. (Certainly any reference to the birth mother as "mother," as advocated by some in open adoption, may severely compromise the child's identification of the "real mother." This is an extremely important area that needs to be researched). But the fantasy life of the adoptee must be taken into account as well.

It was the founder of psychoanalytic theory, Sigmund Freud, who provided us with insights about the fantasy life of a latency-aged child. Every child, he said, whether adopted or biological, has recourse to a particular fantasy when he has suffered hurt upon being reprimanded by his parents. This fantasy, known in the literature as the "family romance," takes root in the idea that the parents with whom he lives are not his "real parents." His "real parents," according to the fantasy, were rich and famous or of noble blood and were somehow separated from the child. They may be "super parents"—never scolding and forever gift-giving. The child believes he will achieve the status in life to which he, of noble ancestry, is entitled. The child resorts to this fantasy whenever he feels frustrated and disappointed by his parents. The fantasy generally is of brief duration and is abandoned once the child realizes that he can both love and hate the same person.

It is important to remember that all children experience these fantasies, which should be regarded as perfectly normal developmental phenomena within the child's psychological growth cycle. All things being equal, the non-adopted child has a slight advantage. Children who live within the security of their biological families can afford the luxury of indulging in the fantasy as a game. For them, it bears no relationship to reality and, therefore, need not be taken too seriously. For the adopted child, however, there is some reality to the fantasy. He may fantasize about the people who brought him into the world, wonder where they are and wonder what they are like as people. The recognition that he was once given up or rejected may be compounded by a sense of dual identification or "genealogical bewilderment." The sense of belonging can be considered more problematic for the adopted child. Parents who struggle continuously with their right to the child may communicate a message that contributes to the child's feeling that he perhaps does not belong to this particular family. That is why it is so important for parents to come to terms with their own feelings about who is the "real parent."

For parents who have resolved their own feelings about biological inadequacy, who can discuss adoption calmly, who love and accept their children regardless of how they came to be part of the family, such fantasies are of little consequence, if any at all. Parents are obliged to truly examine their own feelings about the child and his place in the family. For example, if the parent associates undesirable behavior on the part of the child with "the bad seed" notion, such a parent is vulnerable and may make verbal attacks and innuendoes about the child's "real" parentage, which will cause further breakdown of the parent-child relationship. There are other danger signals as well. If parents view the child, even unconsciously, as a symbol of their biological inadequacy, if the child is used by one or both parents to satisfy their own emotional needs or as a pawn in a marital power struggle, if the parent or parents find themselves fleeing from any discussion of adoption, or if a distrustful or suspicious relationship exists between the child and either parent, then the situation is ripe for faulty resolution of the dilemma which results in a split parental identification.

Considerably more important than the family romance fantasy, from the standpoint of the child's healthy emotional development, is his ability to attain complete identification with his family. The success or failure of this identification, and extent or identification, is dependent on certain variables: the marital relationship, its openness and authenticity, the degree of communication and intimacy between family members, the mutuality of support of members for one another and how the family functions as a unit. The love a child is able to enjoy and express later in life is dependent on the examples provided for him in the matrix of his own family. Issues of intimacy, closeness, trust and hopefulness provide the basis of the adult personality later on in life. This is a lesson we see manifested in countless ways, totally independent of the adoptive theme.

Perhaps the most crucial factor in the psychological development of the child rests in the process known as "identification." Children learn and take on the feelings and attitudes of their parents; i.e., who or what their parents are (including, for the adopted child, his birth parents). The personality of the child is developed through identification with the parents' conscious and unconscious image of the child as one who is loved, and as one who is to be trusted as he learns. Angry orders or suspicions weaken the child's self-esteem, conveys a lack of trust in the child and provides him with an alternative to what he is told to do. The healthy parent is firmly convinced that the child will repress unacceptable impulses; the unhealthy parent does not reflect this confidence—in fact, in many cases, she will predict its occurrence.

The problem of the child's identifying with adoptive parents is that it cannot be done or, at best, is done with some difficulty, if the child hears disparaging or critical remarks about his birth parents. Since part of his identity is tied up with his genetic background, such critical remarks will only serve the purpose of fostering an identification with them. The research evidence seems to suggest that the process of identification is one of the most crucial in the development of the growing child.

Integration of the biological into the environmental context is the lot of every adoptive family. That is why we stress the inclusion of family background information. This includes the demographics of age, height and weight, hair and eye color, complexion, body frame, etc. It should also include any special talents, gifts or deficits inherent in the biological situation. Ideally, it should also contain special interests such as sewing, swimming, reading or the like. We have included a summary form to be used in providing detailed information to the child at given points in his/her growth. Such a form should be completed as soon as possible and kept in a safe place—such as a safety deposit box (see Appendix 2 for example).

Almeda Jolowicz (1969) provides a case example of the effect of the "hidden parent." Paul was a boy born out of wedlock but was never relinquished for adoption. He was placed in several foster homes until he was three years old, at which time, he settled in the one in which he grew up. Throughout the years his mother never visited, the boy never asked about her and it is unclear whether she was even referred to, or how, by the foster parents. The boy seemingly enjoyed a positive relationship with the (foster) parents, but when he reached adolescence, his behavior proved to be increasingly problematic. He refused to do the farm chores required of him and would abruptly leave the farm at will. He let it be known that he no longer had to obey and began to ask a host of questions about his birth mother, a person he could never remember having seen. In desperation, the foster parents requested his replacement (a euphemism in the literature for being kicked out) and there followed a series of unsuccessful placements in other foster homes.

This case illustration, as well as countless others, makes one ask certain questions about the effect of the fantasied parent-child bond. How could a boy who had never known his birth mother be so influenced by her that after ten years of patient and loving care by foster parents result in his complete rejection of them? Are his feelings of having been rejected by his birth mother so strong that he felt he had to do likewise to those who cared for him? Is there something about an original parent-child relationship that gives a parent such mysterious control over a child, even in absentia? Whence comes this power?

To answer some of these questions we must confront a myth that has been perpetuated over the years. That is the mistaken notion that all one needs to do to remove a child from a bad environment to a growth-producing one in order for the latter environment to negate the effects of the former. That may be the way it should work, but it doesn't. The fact of the matter is that each child does have an inner life in which he tries to hold on to the notion that his parents (meaning the people who produced him) were decent, and even honorable, persons. To hear comments to the contrary is objectionable and will certainly lead to a defensive posture on the part of the child. Rather than forgetting about these people, a separation may lead to the idealization of this person or these people. And in the case just cited, one very obvious factor, which necessarily complicated the picture in terms of this boy's sense of identity, was the failure of the agency to obtain a termination of parental rights so this child would be free for adoption. Whether such action would have prevented acting out behavior previously described is academic - but certainly, the foster parents in this case would have felt a greater sense of entitlement to the child than they obviously felt.

This case explains why a given child will identify with adults he has never seen, but fantasized about, through the accounts given him by his adoptive parents. It might be well, at this point, to examine the nature of the process of identification as a vital ingredient in personality development.

A child's personality takes shape as the child learns and accepts the standards and values of his own parents. He learns what behavior is acceptable and what is not, by virtue of the example set for him within the context of a meaningful, growth-producing relationship. The adoptive parent who says, "You're mine despite the fact that someone else gave you birth," tells the child that his "real" family is his adoptive family. If all such messages are this direct and honest, development probably takes place unimpeded. On the other hand, if parents express their disappointment in the child's behavior and relate it to the child's heredity, he receives an unintended message that compromises his place in the family.

There are a number of measures parents can take to solidify the child's identity. Memorabilia in one form or another should be made available to him/her. Photographs taken on the day he came to the family should be placed in his growth book. Every child should have such a book, whether adopted or not. It becomes a part of him. There are, however, children's growth books specifically for adopted children. We do not recommend such books because we believe this draws an undue amount of attention to the fact of adoption.

Another measure to be taken by the parents to solidify the child's identity is through the drawing of a family tree. Family trees have become increasingly popular over the years and, in our view, are a reflection of the current emphasis on roots. Children are frequently asked to draw their own family tree and this presents a dilemma for many adopted children. Knowing that there is another family out there, should he include them—if he does, is he being disloyal to his adoptive family? If he doesn't include them, is he being less than honest with himself and his teacher? There is some controversy over this issue, particular involving those children who were placed later in life and have clear images of their parental past. Other children included in this controversy are biracial or from another country, whose adoptive status is recognizable on sight. Should there be a different set of rules relating to the drawing of a family tree?

As already stated, this is quite a controversial question and the arguments on both sides wax hard and heavy. Barbara Menning, the former director of Resolve stated her position lucidly in a previous newsletter (1982). She stated:

> . . . we are talking about two very previous and totally separate types of identity an adopted child may call his or her heritage; one is the genetic heritage; the other is the upbringing - encom-

passing emotional and physical nurturance, cultural and religious education, and a family complex within which all this happens. We may or may not know much about the genetic heritage of our adopted child. I hope for the day when we will have a great deal of information to share with each child, for I think that is a birthright...My heart aches for the generations of adopted children who have grown up 'genetically anonymous' due to the regulations of agencies, the fears of birth parents and the possessiveness of adoptive couples - all three are guilty of contributing to this violation of human rights (p. 1).

Ms. Menning goes on to state that the adoptive parents part in the child's total self-identity not be obliterated. The care and devotion of the adoptive parents gives them the right to call these children their own and their part in the child's identity in his birthright as well. Pleading for both adoptive and birth parents to quit competing with each other and feeling threatened by the others' existence, she asks that each recognize and appreciate the place of the other on the child's family tree.

Our own position is a bit less absolute. (We do agree, however, that a child has an absolute right to be provided with genetic background data and that such information is vital to his emotional well-being). Our feeling is that how the family tree is drawn depends on a number of factors. It depends on a number of factors. It depends on the age of the child, the meaning of adoption to him, and whether or not the child is transracial. In the case of a child who has lived any length of time (3 or more years), there are permanent memories etched into his mind about these parent figures. One would do the child a disservice by drawing only an adoptive family. The practice might even lead to further resentment on the child's part for his perception of your efforts to get him to disown his original family. In a transracial situation, we suggest your sitting down with him and discussing the importance *he* attaches to his racial heritage, and allow the advice to flow therefrom. Obviously, this is more of a "mixed bag" and certainly, in either case, the parents' attitudes toward the child's genetic family is of critical importance.

As we have stated in our previous publication, however, for a child placed in infancy with no previous imprinting ties to the birth parents and of the same race as the (adoptive) parents, there is really no justification for the inclusion of the genetic family tree. What you are doing (in pushing for the inclusion of the genetic family tree when no need exists to do so) is to inadvertently foster an identification with his genetic forebearers and may further complicate the progress he has made toward the development of his own personal identity. We must always remember that the child's identity takes shape as he learns and accepts the standards and values of his family. As he learns and accepts the behaviors that are acceptable and unacceptable within the context of a meaningful, growth-producing parental relationship, his identity becomes formed. It is not that we are "killing off" the birth parents - their influence is always there. But the child really wants to be part of his new family and takes particular pride in knowing, not only that he is a part of this (adoptive) family but that you want him there and are glad of his presence.

Some adoptive parents use adoption as a means of highlighting the specialness of their family arrangement. Some even celebrate the adoption anniversary as a day of special note. We consider that practice as a rather superfluous gesture and therefore deem it to be unnecessary. We recognize that such a celebration may be received as a source of pride. However, even when well-handled, it focuses too much attention on the adoption. On the

JC'86

other hand, parents must recognize that being adopted is different, and it is a difference that must be accepted as a fact of life, both for the adopters as well as the adoptee.

Up until this time, adoption is viewed in a positive light; i.e., the child has viewed adoption in terms of his wantedness. This leads to a favorable self-image, a view of the self as likeable and lovable. The "what" and the "how" of adoption has been answered. But during the latency stage of development, the most difficult question is posed and demands a response: that is the "why" question. It is at this time that many heretofore well-adjusted children begin to ask questions which may have an unsettling effect on the adoptive parents.

The most grievous error parents can make is to assume their child does not have feelings about being adopted. The questions, "Why was I adopted?", "Was I so undesirable that a decision was made for me to deprive me of my birthright?" may suggest a good deal of anguish about his adoptive status. Such questions are painful, and there is increasing evidence that children between the ages of six and adolescence continually contend with such questions. The realization that one was once given up, or rejected, can be quite a blow to the growing child's developing sense of self-worth.

Our guiding principle is that it is not only beneficial, but necessary to allow the child to express these feelings of hurt and rejection. Children who are allowed to express their hurt are, in the long run, emotionally healthier than children who are unable or unwilling to express their feelings. Once these feelings are expressed, the parent can universalize the emotion by suggesting that all adopted children ask these questions and that it is normal to have and to express such feelings. If necessary, allow the child to express the feeling of rejection, of not being wanted. Allow the child to express the feelings of hurt, but also to help the child put the matter into perspective by suggesting that it wasn't *him/her* that was being rejected but the *responsibility* which she (the birth lady) did not feel ready to accept. It is then, and only then, appropriate for the parent to reassure the child that he is loved and wanted (by his adoptive parents) and that he is as valued as if born to them. A comment by the mother, such as, "I would have been very proud to have had you grow in my body," is appropriate because it is true and because it tends to dilute the child's fantasy of his own undesirability.

Adoptive parents should also recognize, in this connection,

that all children, adopted or not, get angry at their parents from time to time and contend with mixed feelings. This has nothing really to do with adoption, but, because the parents are in an adoptive situation, there may be a tendency to relate the child's behavior to it. Adoptive parents must take caution to be aware of the tendency to perceive all experiences with their children through the adoptive lens. Parents should relate to the feelings the children have without interpreting those feelings as an indictment of the parents.

Dealing specifically with a child's perceived rejection varies with the individuals involved. Honesty is absolutely essential. Parents should not expect to have a single "right" answer. What is said is less important than the feelings of acceptance behind the words. It is important not to be too critical of the birth mother, as this may invite the child to defend her and, hence, to identify too strongly with her. Conversely, it is inadvisable to lavish her with such praise that the child sees her as victimized and distraught over the sacrificial decision that was made.

Middle ground is probably best. The following is an appropriate explanation: "We don't know a great deal about the woman who gave birth to you, but we do know that she found herself in a difficult position and wanted to make the right decision for you. She wanted you to have a better life than she could provide for you, and she found that, through adoption, you could be given a good home with a mother and father who would love you and care for you as she felt you should be cared for. Having made her decision probably before you were born, she was then in a better position to work out her own situation; i.e., go back to school, work, or whatever. She made this decision knowing it was final." By emphasizing that the woman probably made her decision prior to the child's birth, the child is less likely to feel that she took a look at him and decided he was unlovable.

In any explanation, the parent must take care not to stress that the birth mother made her decision out of love. There is really no way of knowing whether love entered the picture. But what we do know is that it was out of a recognition of her inability to provide the right kind of home. If adoption is explained primarily in terms of love, there may always be the fear that the adoptive parent will do likewise since s/he professes to love the child. The important underlying principle is that the adoptive parent must help the child achieve a positive self-image, a feeling that he is good and lovable.

In some cases, parents attempt to over-reassure the child about his worth to the birth mother by reminding the child that she decided against an abortion. We feel this is totally unnecessary. The child will, himself or herself, arrive at this conclusion independently, but for the adoptive parents to bring it up (to reassure the child of his acceptability) is to invoke possible guilt feelings and a sense of obligation toward the birth mother.

Finally, it is important to recognize that the working through of these feelings (rejection, hurt, anger, even guilt) takes a while and that *you cannot rush the process.* In other words, the child must be given time and opportunity to allow his feelings to settle and to come to grips with them. In essence, he must be allowed to grieve the loss, albeit a fantasied loss. As part of this process, there may be fleeting feelings of anger (over the perceived rejection), and the child should be told that all adoptees encounter these feelings from time to time—it is part of the uniqueness of being an adoptee. As parents, we should also realize that we cannot shield our children, that dealing with hurt and disappointment is part of life itself, and that our childrens' encounter of such feelings is not an indictment of how we carry out our role as parents.

This is not to suggest, however, that because the child was once rejected the parent should protect him from any measure of criticism or correction. There is no reason for the parent to feel he or she must make up for the original hurt. We suggest that the parents recognize the hurt and confusion and relate to the child just as if he had been born to them, without special compensatory efforts. To the extent that the parents become good role models for the child and to the extent that he has been accepted and integrated into the fabric of the family, the child's identification will be with the adoptive parent and not with his birth parents. The message to the child that he is a good person, loved and valued for himself and that he will turn out to be a responsible adult is the best guarantee that such will, in fact, eventually come to pass.

The literature on adoption contains many references to the conflicts and identity issues adoptees go through in their developmental years (Triseliotis, 1973; Sorosky, Baran and Pannor, 1975). The following is an illustration of a twelve year old girl who was particularly troubled by her adoptive status. As the middle child and only adopted child in this family, adoption was used divisively by Donna and other family members. In this interview, Donna expresses the confusion and hurt feelings that many adoptees state has been their experience.

Dr. Smith: I am an adoptive parent—two of my three are adopted. But the two who are adopted outnumber the one who isn't. In your case, it's the other way around. I know your sister, Judy, has said things about your being adopted, but I don't know about your brother, Steve.

Donna: He doesn't say anything.

Dr. Smith: He doesn't say anything, but adoption can be used as a weapon, and like you said, it was sort of like "hitting below the belt" with it—things like, "you know you're not my real sister." If Judy were here, I would say - "is that the way you feel, that she's not your real sister?" And what do you think she would say?

Donna: I don't think she really means it. I think it's just a way to get back.

Dr. Smith: It comes out when she's angry—is that right?

Donna: Sometimes she says it when she says she's joking around, but she doesn't know how much it really hurts me.

Dr. Smith: Do you tell her it hurts you?

Donna: She would probably say that, well, "why should it hurt you—you're just an adopted kid—why be any different?" I don't know really what she would say, but the way she acts, it's probably what she would say. Or she would say she really didn't care.

Dr. Smith: Does she understand how different it is to be an adopted child?

Donna: I don't really think she does, because I guess, it's just, I guess you have to really be an adopted child to understand how it feels. There was this kid in school and everything—everybody was, you know, talking about me because I was an adopted child.

And then one of my friends came over and said I know how it feels—and I told her she didn't know how it feels because she wasn't an adopted child, she didn't really have the experience or realize the things that happened to me. I can do the same things as any other child, but I kind of feel out of place because I really want to find out what my parents are like. Well, mom found out some things about my parents—my natural parents—though she said I couldn't find out if I had any brothers or sisters at all and she said it was really against the law and all that and I was kind of upset because I really wanted to know if I had any brothers and sisters.

Dr. Smith: I understand what you mean, but if you saw them on the street, what would you really have in common with them? Would you have any feelings for them?

Donna: Probably not as...no, I don't think so.

Dr. Smith: See, love is something that develops over a long period of time and I guess in a sense it's our hangup with blood that we think that those relationships were more important. But, your mother and father met each other—they probably didn't love each other the first time they saw each other. They may not even have been able to stand each other but the love grew and I get the feeling that they have a pretty close relationship with each other. I guess you have to decide who are your loved ones. You're smiling.

Donna: Well, I know who my real parents are.

Dr. Smith: Who are your real parents?

Donna: My mom and dad that I live with right now.

Dr. Smith: Do you have feelings about this person who gave you up years ago?

Donna: I would probably, if I really knew her as well as I do my mom and dad, I would probably love her just as much, but I'm kind of wondering why she did give me up and if she really did love me, so I don't know.

Dr. Smith: I don't know if she loved you. I don't know if she didn't. Usually the way these situations go is it was very difficult. She found herself in a situation she felt she couldn't handle and she wanted you to have the best kind of family life that anybody could give you and so she made that decision. But I don't know what her feelings were about that. Do you think your fantasy is that she's hurting over this decision that she made?

Donna: No, I don't really think so.

Dr. Smith: Do you have a fantasy that she is glad about this decision she made? What does your fantasy tell you about this woman...or are you thinking about a woman and a man?

Donna: Well, I'm just wondering what they really look like and what I'm really worried about is if they had health problems or anything...

Dr. Smith: Health problems?

Donna: Yeah, like I really wanted to know if they had a problem, if they ever had a case history of like, some sort of disease and I was afraid that they might pass it on to me. Mom and dad thought that I was really trying to get back at them but I wasn't. I just was trying to find out if I'd be healthy or if any changes would happen to me or if I'd be really tall or I'd be short or something.

Dr. Smith: I think those are very natural questions. Questions about what they look like, how tall they were, what color hair, what color eyes, what kind of allergies, what kind of family diseases there were, if there was diabetes in the family. Those are all very natural questions. Did your parents say they wouldn't be able to get that kind of information?

Donna: They didn't say.

Dr. Smith: Well, let me...I can talk to them about this. Suppose I tried to get some information from the agency as much as they have and share that with you. Would you want me to do that?

Donna: Well, I found some things that my mom brought home.

Dr. Smith: Really?

Donna: Yeah, I found out that my natural mother, not the mother I'm with now, but that she had polio when she was six and mono when she was in high school.

Dr. Smith: Mono when she was in high school? Anything else?

Donna: No, I guess not.

Dr. Smith: I think you have a right to this genetic heritage and you know, to the extent that this information is available and if your parents aren't able to, I can write to the agency and they can send it to me and I can share that with you. But, I think what you've got to do is come to terms with the idea that this woman, for whatever reason, made that decision and I mean, could you live with it? I think it's very unfortunate that adoption can be used as a weapon in a family . . . either by you or by your parents or your brothers or sisters. See, this is not to say that what we do is right, but we have this rule that adoption is not used as a way to get somebody else to do something they don't want to. It's just a standard rule. I mean, two of my kids are adopted. But, so what? That doesn't give them any special privileges, and it doesn't give them any special deficits either. There is no way they can use that to their advantage or disadvantage. We're their parents and they're our children and the way they came to us is almost immaterial. At the same time, it's okay to realize that there's a difference and that's what I want to talk to you about. What are your feelings about being an adopted child? Is it harder, is it more difficult? Do you wish maybe you weren't adopted?

Donna: Well, sometimes when my parents . . . I guess I just

try to get back at them with a little bit of my adoption and I get...I'm sort of happy that they...I think about the reasons like maybe my mother, my natural mother, didn't have too many things like you said and I'm happy that they did give me somebody who could really care for me better than they could but sometimes I kind of wonder whether it was really the right choice because I sometimes wonder whether my parents really did love me and I always say to myself, "Well, I don't know why my natural father and mother had to give me up."

Dr. Smith: It bothers you that the decision was made to give you up?

Donna: Sometimes, some of it.

Dr. Smith: If they hadn't given you up do you have any fantasies of what your life would be like?

Donna: No. I don't know. If...I would probably be living...I was born in another city and I guess I might just live there and might totally live the same way they do...and most of the people in my natural family are tall and I don't know. I would probably look more like them and people wouldn't always be asking why I don't look like my mon and dad and everything.

Dr. Smith: That bugs you when they keep commenting on that, is that right?

Donna: Yeah. I remember one time when this one lady came over to our house. I think she was our piano teacher. I was sitting next to my sister, I mean next to the piano, listening to her play and then, after the thing the lady came up to me and said, "It's really nice of you to come over and listen to Judy." And then she went over to Judy and said, "You sure have nice friends," and then she said, "She's is my sister." And she said, "You don't look a thing like her." That kind of made me upset that I can't look like the rest of my family but I think now I see that nobody really looks exactly like anybody else.

Dr. Smith: I think sometimes people make remarks that do hurt, that are very tactless, that shows their insensitivity. But I don't think they mean to hurt. I think it's what I call our "hangup with blood." You know, people are always making remarks that "blood is thicker than water," "he's a chip off the old block," "he inherited the personality characteristics of that person." That's a lot of nonsense. The fact is, you will turn out to be the kind of person that, within reason, your parents are. Because it's the environment. I guess my question to you is, do you think they love you?

Donna: I really do, but I wonder, I do wonder. I see them, I don't know if it's true but sometimes I see them paying a little more attention to Judy because she's younger and Steve because he's older. I feel kind of like the middle child, like I'm right smack dab in the middle and if I get blamed for anything it's because she's younger and the baby of the family and he's older and he's maturing more and he's little bit older than I am. I'm right in the middle of those two. And I know they get in trouble as much as I do but I kind of feel that I'm not. . .I guess it's the same with Judy and Steve. I think Judy feels she's the baby, she doesn't get the same things as I do. I get more. I guess I get more responsibility.

Dr. Smith: Yeah, I agree. In fact, I told your parents this. In some ways you are very unique because you are the middle child, okay? And that's rough. It is also rough in that your sister came into the world 14 months after you did. So, you just got used to them and you had to share them. Not that you remember that. But it is also rough being the only adopted child. Now I think it is also important not to use that as some sort of a leverage to either make them prove that they love you as much as they love Judy and Steve. In other words, I think you have got to accept the adoption as a fact of life and ask "do I really belong to this family?" If you come to that decision, that this is the family you really belong to, then let's forget about adoption. You know, let's go on and live our life and be happy. If communication is a problem between you and your parents, then let's talk about it.

Donna: Well, it's partly my fault because I am usually all by myself. Like on Sunday dinner and we're all together, I usually go off and eat by myself. I'm trying to eat with them but sometimes they bring up subjects or fights and they start fighting right in the middle of it and then I get caught in the fight and everybody gets upset and they bring up things that I don't really want to talk about. They always ask me questions all the time, always suspicious that I'm doing something wrong and I guess...I don't know. I guess I'm a loner, I just like being all by myself most of the time. I don't like big groups, being in big groups. When I'm in big groups I don't think I can handle it. I don't like being around a whole lot of people at one time. I know there are only five in my family but I like just sitting by myself and eating. I guess thinking things out by myself or just sitting there by myself for a little while and when I'm talking to my friends I can't have a big crowd around me. I'll talk to one person. Sometimes I just like walking by myself or playing games by myself.

Dr. Smith: I guess what I'm reacting to or what I'm hearing you say is that you do feel by yourself but I also get the flavor of your feeling that you've been abandoned.

Donna: Well, I don't really feel abandoned because it's mostly I go off and do it myself, but...

Dr. Smith: Yeah, but where do you feel you belong? Do you feel like you don't know where you belong?

Donna: It's really like I don't know where I belong. I don't know what...

Dr. Smith: And do you think maybe it's because you're struggling with the idea of having been given up?

Donna: I kind of feel like they really didn't want me. It's

like, and then I feel like mom and dad felt sorry for seeing a little baby...I don't know. And then I feel kind of privileged because I was among all these other babies and they picked me out of all of them. That's what everybody says. You know, you're so privileged. It's not really being privileged because you get caught with all the worries and hassles and they think it's really neat to be adopted because you get the privilege.

Dr. Smith: They don't know that there is a side of being adopted where it hursts, right?

Donna: I guess it's like you have to be there. I mean, it's like you have to have the experience. They think it's so neat and that you're different, you start believing them. And then I guess you start believing yourself you're so different. People think it's so neat to be different so you just try to please them and be different.

Dr. Smith: Do you ever get the message that people say that you should be grateful that they rescued you from a bad situation?

Donna: Yes, because, they say you could have just been left there or something like that or you're lucky.

Dr. Smith: Who says that?

Donna: Well, they ask me like when they found out I was adopted, they said...some of my friends said you're very lucky—it's very lucky that you got picked. I mean it's not—they said I was very lucky to be picked by such a nice family. That makes me feel good that they think my family is nice but what makes me so lucky. But it also makes me feel bad, that I had to be saved.

Dr. Smith: Or that you were undesirable? Is that the feeling? Do you ever have the fantasy that your birth mother took one look at you and said, "I don't want this kid?"

Donna: That's what I thought at first.

Dr. Smith: At first?

Donna: But, I guess it's been with me ever since I was a child. I guess I've had that feeling.

Dr. Smith: What if I told you that in all probability, and I think this is the case, in all probability she made her decision before you were even born. In other words, she could not have seen you, but that it was the situation she found herself in that she felt she wanted to make a decision that was going to be helpful to you.

Donna: I remember thinking to myself and I said maybe she—I asked my mon and dad if they had become like, like she was going to give me up in the first place like when she was during her pregnancy and mom and dad just got me back, like before. But then I realized that I wasn't . . . they hadn't really talked to the mother or anything or talked to anybody and they told me they didn't, they got me just out of seeing and, so, I thought maybe she just wanted to give me up because . . . I really can't explain it but like . . . just like you said, like she took one look at me . . .

Dr. Smith: That's your fantasy; she took one look at you?

Donna: I don't know if it's a fantasy. Some of the time I wish that, it's true I have to be honest with you, sometimes I do wish she hadn't really given me up. I wish she had really taken me. Sometimes I really wish that for a small while I could spend a little time with her. If I did that, I know I'd be hurting my mom and dad and I really don't want to do that, I really don't. I really think they love me too much.

Dr. Smith: And at the same time, it hurts you that she gave you up . . .

Donna: I probably will never see her.

Dr. Smith: In other words, that you are really experiencing a rather severe loss. You feel you lost something.

Donna: Yes, I remember one time I was talking to my friend and I told her I had two sets of parents...that it was really neat that I could go see sometime I could go see my other parents and spend time with them, but then I knew it wasn't true. I knew I could never see them.

Dr. Smith: I think you should know that all adopted children wonder what these people are like, what they look like, what they are as people; because part of what you are is tied up with them. Now, I think that at some point in your life you will be able to decide, you know, if you actually want to look them up. What I advise people to do, and I tell my own kids this too, you know, that's an important decision that only you can make when the time comes. But, you know, it's one thing to be so curious and having that need that's so great that if you go to look them up, are you willing to face the consequences, whatever that is. In other words, this mother may not want to see you and may be upset with that visit. She may say, "Well, I don't know who you are," she may deny the whole thing or she may say, "Well, I did have a child but the child has her own home, her own family, and I look at you as a total stranger." You know, that's why I think a lot of adoptees feel that, look, a decision has been made which supposedly was in my best interest. Why upset the decision that she made, you know, 20 years ago. I am not trying to talk you into it or out of it, Donna, I think that there are things to be said on both sides. And, I am also saying that I can see where that part of the experience hurt. And, I think being a teenager is hard regardless of whether you're adopted or not.

Donna: I guess it would really be up to her because I guess it was her decision in what she decided. I guess I'd have to live with that. Since I have to live with that, I guess I'll have to cope with it and I'll have to work it out and I guess with the help of my family I really can work it out and I won't use it as a weapon

against my family as an excuse. But it's just like trying to quit smoking...it takes time.

Dr. Smith: You know what I also see in your eyes? I see a lot
of hurt that the decision was made. I think that kind
of hurt is natural. I am sorry you hurt, Donna. And,
I'm sorry people have used adoption as a weapon
against you and I am sorry you had to feel that you
had to use it to throw a dig at your parents. But
nobody can say that you have to belong to this
family. I think that's a decision you have to make.
"Who are my real parents? Are my real parents the
ones who brought me into the world or are my real
parents the ones who cared for me, nurtured me,
cried over me when I was sick...who are my real
parents?" And, that's a decision you will have to
make.

Donna: I guess the definition of parents is what you said,
really taking care of me. That makes me feel good.

This case illustrates the mixture of feelings many adoptees
verbalize. The first thing this case illustrates is the tremendous
variation of responses and reactions adoptees experience and there
is no body of knowledge which presupposes a universality of
response. Secondly, even though this family was somewhat typical
of other adoptive families, it was unfortunate that adoption was
allowed to be used as a weapon, both by family members and
by Donna, herself. The reader may be interested in knowing that
Donna has now accepted her place in her "new" family but that
before she was able to do so, she had to (belatedly) work through
the angry and struggling feelings with which she was contending.
Also, the rules for allowing her to isolate herself from her family
have been altered so that this behavior is no longer allowed. In
essence, both she and other family members have truly accepted
Donna's real place in the family.

Adopted children, as all children, have certain rights. Dr.
Barbara Stilwell, a psychiatrist in private practice, recently
delineated these rights most poignantly for the adopted child.

"I have a right to be wanted...by at least one adult...and preferably two. I want to be wanted very intensely because I have been rejected at a very tender age...for perhaps a very necessary and even inevitable reason. Because of that rejection, I am particularly vulnerable to feelings of disillusionment and abandonment. In order to develop human trust, I need to feel especially secure with the generous adults who have chosen to adopt me.

"I have a right to expediency in adoption...because I desperately need continuity of care. It will give me a security that will make my whole development flow more smoothly. I won't be afraid to grow.

But don't adopt me before you are ready; preparation is mandatory before I cross the threshold of your home. Part of that preparation is grieving: Yes, grieving the loss of your procreative function or that of your spouse's. It's a great loss, you know, like losing a family member, or a job, or a limb, or some other vital function. It requires times to absorb the loss...time to work through the various stages of grief; denial, depression, anger and acceptance. It won't go smoothly...one, two, three, four. There will be times you think you're over it, and then you'll cry all the next day. There will be times you will rage with anger and blame any source you can think of. There will be times of numbness and indifference. But you will work it through...and then you'll be ready to commit yourself to me.

"The other part of preparation is the exciting part. Remember ... natural parents have nine months of preparatory excitement. I expect you to read books, go shopping for baby furniture, talk your head off and hold every baby that comes within sight. And, by the time that phone call comes to tell you I'm on my way, I expect you to be cool as a cucumber, because ...

"I have a right to parents who are free of overwhelming anxiety. I know you don't know just how to hold me ... or how to decipher my messages of need ... or how to respond to my every cry. But you'll learn ... if you're confident and committed ... and have the support of helping people.

"When you commit yourself to me, I want you to realize you are taking a risk! I may not fulfill your fantasies of what a child should be. Just as I may be bald-headed and cross-eyed in infancy, I may later show some real defects that can't be identified in infancy. Remember ... if I were a natural child, you would be taking risks, too. With adoption you are taking a few more. There is no way I can come to your home with a guarantee of beauty, creative talents and an I.Q. of 140. I'm just a human being. I have a right to be accepted for what I am.

"And if I do turn out to have a major defect . . . I expect you to grieve . . . just like any other loss . . . denial, depression, anger, acceptance. It's a part of life.

"Do I want to know that I'm adopted? Sure, when I'm able to understand the information. I will develop different levels of understanding at different ages. Make sure you don't give me more information than I want to know. Brief, simple answers will always suffice until I ask another question. And for goodness sakes, don't give me that gushy 'chosen child' stuff. I'm awfully big-headed as a child, anyway. If you feed me a fantasy that I am special, I'll think I deserve unlimited privileges and may behave like a real 'monster.' It will be much harder for me to contain my aggression if I think I'm a 'privileged character.'

"Many children have fantasies that they have another set of parents somewhere who are superhuman beings. They 'give presents, never discipline and never say no to anything.' These fantasies arise when a child becomes angry at his parents. They dissipate when a child learns that he can love and hate the same person. As an adopted child I may prolong this fantasy because the first half of it is true. I do have a 'real' mom and dad somewhere. If my parents don't rear me with realistic limit setting and help me keep my feelings about love and hate integrated, I'll make that fantasy grow as tall as the biggest windmill.

"The flip side of that fantasy record is that I'm a no-good reject. It carries such imagery as 'my mother was a slut or my father a runaway drunken bum.' If I rely on that imagery, I don't ever have to expect much from myself . . . because I was never anything worthwhile to being with. As an adoptive parent you must be calm about my background and rear me with positive attitudes and messages. If you are uneasy about my background and continuously see the 'evil' in me, I'll develop an impermeable, negative self-concept that no psychotherapeutic sledgehammer can crack. I must learn that I am a summation of all my experiences, not just my genealogical roots.

"And when the age of maturity comes . . . , and I have an interest in my genealogical roots, I have the right to pursue them. My young adult ego strives for identity; I have a right to a sense of history in working out that identity; I have a right to a sense of history in working out that identity. Camouflage and intrigue build fantasies; truth builds a sense of reality.

"I need parents who have a deep respect for each other. Like natural children, I will develop oedipal strivings. I'll have times of wanting an exclusive relationship with my parent of the opposite sex and a desire to force my same-sexed parent out of the relationship. If my parents' marriage is in jeopardy, that fantasy may come too close to coming true. I must not be used by one parent to control the other. I am not a channel of communication. I have no childhood degree in family relations. I cannot come into a home to solve marital strife. I need parents who know how to love each other.

" I need parents who can share their love with me. Some parents are too exclusive with their love. I know an adopted girl who felt so rejected by her parents' love for each other that her greatest desire was to have a baby so she could create her own loving relationship. Other adolescents turn to a sexual relationship too soon out of the same motivation. I need a parent-child relationship that is as loving as the marital relationship.

"I have a right to be loved just for myself . . . not because I am a banner of social cause. If I am interracial, I want to grow up in an environment that will tolerate me with my mixed identity. I want to be around others who are like me. I am not an issue; I am a person. I need a community of friends who will accept me.

"I do not want to be an experiment for parents who may have failed in previous parenting experiences. I have a right to parents who are free of mental illness. I cannot be a cure for someone's neurosis.

"Lastly, I have a right to parents who keep on growing. When the adoption is 'closed,' the job has just begun. I have a right to parents who will counsel, read, attend classes and do everything possible to keep in tune with my developmental expectations and needs. I need parents who will get me help if I need it, without feeling they have failed. My psychological growth is made more complex by adoption, and I want every opportunity to grow up healthy, happy and proud."*

*From an address given by Barbara Stilwell, M.D., titled "The Emotional Rights and Needs of the Adopted Child—As Voiced by a Child" on April 20, 1976 at a symposium titled "Major

Dilemmas in Neonatal Pediatrics." (Reprinted with permission of the author).

Retelling the adoption story may be difficult for the parents, but you should remember that your child is now able to deal with it at a higher level of abstraction and show feelings about the fact of his status. In attempting to relate your feelings of love to the child, as well as your presumed understanding of the birth parents' motivation to release the child for adoption, it is best to convey your own understanding of the nature of love. The notion of "love at first sight" is undoubtedly a myth in most instances. The child should not be taught that love in any relationship occurs instantaneously. Love is something that is nurtured and deepens as people live and share meaningful experiences with each other.

It may be difficult to discuss adoption with a child without implying that he was rescued from inadequate parents. The difficulty arises, in part, from the problems adoptive parents who wanted a child so badly themselves have in identifying with parents who relinquish their child. Birth parents must be accepted for themselves as people, without judgment for their actions, lest criticism of them gives the child the impression that she/he, too, is being criticized. The perception of unacceptability must be changed through assurances that the child is, indeed, wanted. The most important thing for adoptive parents to recognize is that the child wants to know not how he got here, but whether his parents are glad that he is here.

The adopted child must be assured there are positive as well as negative aspects of his situation. His feelings of loss and rejection can be countered by stressing his desirability and goodness. Certainly, the recognition that he was and is wanted can lead him to a healthy self-concept.

CHAPTER 8

THE ADOPTED ADOLESCENT

The literature on the psychology of adolescence points to an inescapable salient fact: adolescence is a troublesome time of life when self-doubts and searching questions are the rule rather than the exception. For the adopted child, problems encountered in adolescence can make the search for self-identity even more difficult, particularly if the child's relationship with the parents is strained or if his or her identification with them is tentative or incomplete.

That period of life we refer to as adolescence is fraught with mixed feelings for both the adolescent as well as his parents. To the adolescent it represents, on the one hand, an end of parental domination, or at least a diminution of parental control, but on the other hand, it calls for increased responsibility and decision-making regarding future roles and goals (which in and of itself is considerably anxiety producing). At the same time, s/he views this period of life with a certain mystique and intrigue regarding his own future romantic life and experiences. This, too, arouses both pleasure and apprehension. To the parent whose children have reached the adolescent years, s/he wonders how stormy the familial environment will become, and muses over the implications that his son or daughter is now a "man" or a "woman." As James Anthony accurately pointed out, if the adult remembers how much of her/himself went into the making of an adolescent, s/he would be better able to understand the complexities of the changed relationship between parent and adolescent (1969). The matter was well summed up by a Hebrew sage in 1230: "Your son at 5 is your master, at 10 your slave, at 15 your double, and after that, your friend or foe, depending on how you brought him up." In short, the period we refer to as adolescence, a period which symbolically represents a rite of passage from childhood, is viewed by all ages with both positive and negative feelings. Certainly in the light of our "sexual revolution," there are grounds for concerns about adolescent renunciation of traditional personal and family sexual values and standards.

Many adolescents turn to literature as a way of expressing and reflecting their confused and, at times, tormented state of existence. But not all adolescents experience the sense of turbulence that the literature would have us believe is universal. Many view it as a mixture of sorrow and joy, anxieties and expectations. One young man, in thinking about these transitory years, stated the following:

> "Before me stood the massive, three-story building complex with its maze of unexplored halls, its musty-smelling shops, its gym, its band rooms, and huge auditorium. And here I stood ten years ago, one lonely, insecure, terrified 12 year old boy facing his first day at junior high school. My former warm, secure, sheltered and protected social matrix which revolved around home, school, neighborhood and church would, in the near future, be rapidly replaced by an impersonal, demanding, competitive and often lonely matrix where only the strongest survive and where I would be forced to cope with and adjust to pressures and expectations in order to avoid being bypassed by the system. This one day in my life—my first day as a junior high school student—stands out in my mind as a sign post symbolizing the rites of passage from childhood to adolescence and marked the first step in the gradual maturational process which eventually leads to adulthood."*

This is a time of life that should be viewed as a transitional period rather than behavior that remains fixed. Adolescence is essentially an in-between stage, with no special rights and privileges of its own, and which forms the basis of the need to examine and re-examine what his purpose and destiny in life is meant to be.

Parents should realize that the adolescent is primarily a child and not an adult, except in a biological sense. Emotionally s/he is still as dependent on his parents as always. However, hormonal changes and societal demands propel him to claim her/his independence, assertions which probably can never be met. The wise parents would do well not to force the youngster to carry out his or her claim to that effect. The parent should always allow the

---

*Author unknown.

youngster to retreat and "save face," recognizing the fact that we have all spoken foolishly and irresponsibly from time to time.

Another characteristic of adolescent phenomena is extreme idealism. The adolescent finds the adult world full of contradictions. For those adolescents who have observed inconsistencies in his parents, or adult behaviors which do not jibe with their avowed stances, his own value framework may be undergoing change and heightened anxiety. The way s/he may deal with such conflicts is to identify even more with his peer group who, s/he perceives, is experiencing similar phenomena with their own parents.

The transition from childhood to adulthood may be a rather sudden shift or it may occur gradually in a setting where children and adults are not sharply separated groups. In situations or societies in which children and adults constitute clearly defined groups, the adolescent does not wish to belong any longer to the children's group and at the same time s/he knows that s/he is not really accepted in the adult group. In this case s/he has a position similar to what is called in sociology "marginal man."

To discuss adolescence in its widest ramifications, that is, physiologically, metabolically, psychologically, anthropologically, developmentally, etc. would be beyond the scope of this book, but one writer has added such insights into our understanding, which is particularly relevant to the adoptive situation, that his genius simply cannot be ignored. One of the most prolific writers of our day, Erik Erikson has shed unmatched insight into our understanding of the adolescent (as well as other phases of development). Erikson added the dimension of cultural influences on personality within an already existing sophisticated psychoanalytic perspective. His contributions, it seems, complement rather than supplant psychoanalytic theory, which further speaks to his genius.

According to Erikson, the central problem of the adolescent is the establishment of a sense of identity. The identity the adolescent seeks to clarify is who he is and what his role in society is to be. Is he a child or an adult? Does he have the wherewithal to be a good husband and father some day? Will his race or religion prevent him from reaching his tentative goals? Overall, will he be a success or failure? By reason of the questions he poses to himself, the adolescent is sometimes morbidly preoccupied with how he appears in the eyes of others as compared with his own self-images and how he can make the roles and skills learned earlier conform with what is currently in style.

Perhaps because of our success-oriented culture, Erikson states that it is the inability to select an appropriate occupational identity that disturbs young people:

To keep themselves together they temporarily over identify, to the point of apparent complete loss of identity, with the heroes of cliques and crowds. On the other hand, they become remarkably clammish, intolerant and cruel in their exclusion of others who are "different", in skin color or cultural background. . . arbitrarily as *the* signs of an in-grouper or out-grouper. It is important to understand such intolerance as the necessary defense against a sense of identity diffusion, which is unavoidable at a time of life when the body changes its proportions radically . . . when intimacy with the other sex approaches and is, on occasion, forced on the youngster, and when life lies before one with a variety of conflicting possibilities and choices. Adolescents help one another temporarily through such discomfort by forming cliques and by stereotyping themselves, their ideals and their enemies (pp. 218–219).

Viewed from this perspective in a culture which extols, above all other considerations "success," the compensatory drives of adolescence can readily be understood. To the adolescent, what represents strength takes precedence over what is evidence of true or mature strength. The adolescent needs to feel powerful, to obliterate all possible rivals, and to rely for such purposes on fantasies of omnipotence.

Summarizing the phenomenon of adolescence is a herculean task, but we like the statement of Anna Freud best. She stated (1958):

I take it that it is normal for an adolescent to behave for a considerable length of time in an inconsistent and unpredictable manner; to fight his impulses and to accept them; to ward them off successfully and to be overrun by them; to love his parents and to hate them; to revolt against them and to be dependent on them; to be deeply ashamed to acknowledge his mother before others and, unexpectedly, to desire heart to heart talks with her; to thrive on imitation of and identification with others while searching unceasingly for his own identity; to be more idealistic, artistic, generous, and unselfish than he will ever be again, but also the opposite; self-centered, egotistic, calculating. Such fluctuations between extreme opposites would be deemed highly abnormal at any other time of life. At this time they may signify no more than that an adult structure of personality takes a long time to emerge, that the ego of the individual in question does not cease to experiment and is in no hurry to close down on possibilities. If the temporary solutions seem abnormal to the

> onlooker, they are less so, nevertheless, than the hasty deci-
> sions made in other cases for onesided suppression, or revolt,
> or flight, or withdrawal, or regression, or asceticism, which are
> responsible for the truly pathological development described
> above (pp. 275–276).

If adolescents living with their biological parents suffer from a crisis identity, the confusion faced by the adopted child is compounded by the fact that he has been exposed to the knowledge that he does have birth parents. The genealogical questions become paramount as he learns about reproduction and childbearing, particularly at a time in our history when there is heightened awareness of the genetic aspects of functioning, as, for example, his intellectual endowment. Reactions to adolescence may vary, as it will in all adolescents. He may deny the existence of some traits he believes are inherited. The degree to which he works out such conflicts is directly related to the success the adoptive parents have had in conveying the message that he is one of them in every sense of the word; i.e., the entitlement issue has been adequately resolved.

The adolescent adoptee has a legitimate right to question her/his ancestral roots. Such questioning does not imply that the parents have somehow failed the child. It is characteristic of all adolescents, adopted *and* biological, to question and even reject parental standards in preference to peer standards. This behavior should be viewed with the calm willingness to discuss anything of concern to the adolescent. Keeping the lines of communication open is vital to healthy resolution of some of the universal interpersonal tensions characteristics of the adolescent years.

If the adolescent has questions about genetic or hereditary characteristics, and if the adoptive parents have access to such knowledge, the information should be made available to the adoptee. Generally, the adolescent is curious about what his birth parents looked like and what kind of lifestyles they led, rather than names, place and date of birth, etc.

Ultimately, conflicts do arise and tension is inevitable. Arguments over whether the adoptive or birth parents are the "real" parents can be used as a weapon by either the adolescent or the parent. Children may use any weapons available to them in battles with their parents. The adopted child simply has one more in his arsenal. When the adolescent strikes out angrily, saying, "I don't have to listen to you, you aren't my real parents anyway," the most appropriate response may be to let the matter drop without further comment (but not give in). Then, when cooler heads prevail, comment on the use made by your adolescent of the fact of adoption. This form of metacommunication, i.e., an analysis of the nature of communication between two people, can be quite valuable in averting future non-productive encounters. You might say, "We have cared for you as if you were our birth child and our feelings for you are the same as if you were born to us. We will not let you use the adoption as a way to control us. We don't use it and we don't feel it is fair for you to use it." Such communication lets the adolescent know that his feelings are understandable and that his relationship with his parents is a special one. The message reaffirms that he is, indeed, the adopted parents' child.

The handling of such volative situations is extremely important. Resolution of such issues, in our point of view, depends upon the pre-existing nature of the relationship between adoptive parents and their children. It is crucial that such a potentially explosive situation be handled with honesty and sincerity. By adolescence, the child's power of perception is acute. Because adolescents are sensitive to mixed messages, insincerity and hypocrisy, it is vital that the adoptive parent recognize his/her own feelings before attempting to reassure the child about his/her origins. For example, any feelings of competitiveness and/or anger (even envy) should be acknowledged to oneself. If not acknowledged, these feelings will emerge in your communication with the adolescent as there is no way to disguise it.

Adopters invariably ask child care experts about adoptees' searches for their birth parents. Parents should realize that interest on the part of their children to find out more about their heritage may be a function of mixed and often multiple motivations. Some are curious only about looks and physical characteristics of birth parents, as well as disease proneness. Others are obsessed with the notion of their genetic forebears, and their interest is tied to a need to determine one's psychological identity. Parents should recognize that it is only natural for adolescents to wonder about who they look like and, having missed out on this opportunity, to once again ask the question, "Why?"

As stated earlier, the sealed record controversy is one of the most hotly debated issues in contemporary child caring practices.

There are legal and constitutional questions involved, centering once again on the "equal protection" clause and other passages of the Constitution of the United States. The legalities of the issue have resulted in a modified view of sound adoption practices. In December of 1976, the Child Welfare League of America, the national standard-setting agency in the child welfare field, expressed a modified view. The League reaffirmed its belief in the principle of confidentiality as a value to the birth parents, adoptee and adoptive parents. It recognized, however, that firm and absolute assurances of confidentiality over an extended period of time may not be realistic. Inasmuch as there is mounting pressure to change the laws regarding anonymity and confidentiality (with respect to birth records), the day may come when an adoptee, in a given state, will exercise the right to learn of the identity of his birth parents (1976). (A more comprehensive treatment of this issue is provided in subsequent chapters of this book.)

On the point of the search, parents should recognize that their children have a right to question. Parents should view the questioning with an open mind and identify with the child's curiosity by indicating the naturalness of such questioning. Adoptive parents *should not* (one might even say must not) interpret the adolescent's questions as a rejection of them as parents. Depending on the nature of the questions, our advice is to let the child know that, such questions are universal and that they are welcome matters for discussion. If they are questions about physical and medical characteristics, we can provide you with these data to the extent that we have them. If, on the other hand, you actually want and need to find this person (or persons), we will, at the time of your majority, help you think through the many different facets of this decision. Some birth parents may welcome such an inquiry but others may view it as an intrusion. But you should wait until you are ready, and you should be ready to accept the consequences of such an encounter. In other words, if you met the woman who delivered you, think through ahead of time what you would actually say to her. This position gives the adoptee the freedom to make his or her own decision.

In a well-known study of 52 adult adoptees in England, whose adjustment ranged from excellent to poor, certain important findings emerged. The study revealed that the adolescent adoptee does encounter specific problems in adolescence which are unique to adoptees. These situations arise in four main areas: (1) Learning about adoption; (2) Complications in the normal adolescent process regarding the search for identity: (3) Relationships with adoptive parents may be influenced by the parents' attitude to all of the facets of adoptions, and; (4) Reactions to parental attitudes about any discussion of adoption. What the study revealed is that every child in his life is likely to learn that he/she is adopted and this can happen in a large number of ways not even considered possible by their parents. For example, children who have not been told of adoption noticed even the slightest parental embarrassment if this were displayed when, for example, a birth certificate was required for school, employment and the like. Others detected subtle nuances in conversation between adults and it is an important point to remember that children are particularly sensitive to such subtle cues. Having made such a discovery, that is, of his adoption or of the fact of his adoption, the child or adolescent will not necessarily communicate this understanding to the parents. Of those in the study who learned initially from an outside source that they might have been adopted (65%), only 50% asked their parents if this were true. The others did not even mention it, saying to themselves, "If there is anything to it, my mother will tell me." They were all emphatic that the source of information about adoption should be their parents and by this they meant their adoptive mother. Secondly, in their search for identity, it is with the adoptive parents that adopted adolescence primarily identify. In the 52 cases studied, almost all, however, wanted some factual information about their biological parents; that is, about their age and occupation, something about their personality, and also about why and how they had been placed for adoption. There was, however, a difference when looking at the reaction of boys and girls. The boys tended to be less curious about adoption than girls, but when the boys subsequently married, their wives became curious. Where there was insecurity in the adoptive home and where only fragments of information about biological parents had been given, the frustration caused by withholding such information accentuated feelings of insecurity.

The third facet of this report related to the adolescent's relationship with his adoptive parents. Among those who are well-adjusted, there was evidence of great devotion to and concern for them. For those who are poorly adjusted, there was evidence of marked ambivalence or excessive devotion coupled with resentment that they were thus tied by conscience and feelings of duty. In this latter group there were those who, although desperate to escape from home, stayed at home to care, for example, for parents who are invalids commenting "I felt I owed it to them." There were cases, also, of excessive rebelliousness leading to social deviation and delinquency or to leaving home.

The final area for consideration are parents' attitudes about discussing adoption. Telling a child about his/her adoptive status has traditionally been viewed as problematic for many adoptive parents. It related to their doubts about their own adequacy as parents, and their fear that their children would love them less once they knew that they were not their biological children. An additional concern was that they might want to seek out their birth parents. Nevertheless, new and emerging data suggest that these fears are unfounded and that many adopters view the telling in a much more favorable light, rather than the defensive posture previously identified.

An interview with a young adult adoptee, focusing largely on her recollection of her own adolescence, serves to dramatize the points contained thus far.

Q. Do you think growing up as an adoptee is harder than growing up as a non-adoptee?
A. I'm not sure. I don't think so.

Q. You don't think there's any difference?
A. There's a difference, but I'm not sure it's any more difficult. There are just some different things you have to work through as far as people not understanding what adoption is, but as far as the normal development that everyone goes through, I don't think I was affected in any negative way or that it is any more difficult.

Q. When you say there are some things to work through, could you elaborate on that?
A. You are a little different, and nobody likes to be different from anyone else. So, you have to understand that, yes, I am different, but it's not necessarily bad to be different. In my instance, I think it was very good to be adopted and that's how it was always viewed. Now, that's not always the case. Some of the kids I ran into who found out that they were adopted associated something bad or negative with that.

Q. Is part of the difference having to deal with the sense that one was once given up?

A. I didn't think of it that way until I was a teenager. I just never thought of it in that sense until I really understood what childbearing was all about. I wondered why, but I just left it.

Q. You don't remember asking your parents the question "why?"

A. No. I think implicitly it was understood, but I don't ever recall asking the question, except facially or nonverbally. When they said something about adoption, I thought maybe I had a question mark on my face and they would say someone thought we could take better care of you than he or she could. But, actually, in terms of an explicit question, no, that didn't happen. I just accepted it, and I remember hearing that at a pretty young age.

Q. My impression of you is that you are, essentially, a healthy person, you have good peer relationships and that you have developed a fairly good sense of your own personal and social competence. In other words, it strikes me that you have a pretty good view of yourself and that you think of yourself in basically positive terms. Has it always been that way?

A. No. Its' had its ups and downs. I feel good about myself when I'm in tune with other people. Other people are very important to me; and, if I'm isolated or feel all alone or I'm not very happy, then I don't feel so good. In those cases, I might be tempted to feel sorry for myself and say "somebody dumped me," or words to that effect. Other times I was angry with my parents and I didn't feel good. I'm not sure that that would be any different than what goes on in the life stages of all people. At times, we all wonder if we are really okay or not. I think as I got older my confidence has increased. There were some things not related to adoption. Our family moved a lot when I was young and that doesn't help when you really don't have any place to call home. You're always having to make new friends. That can be a negative experience. For a while I got sick of being the new kid. That really didn't have anything to do with adoption, and it's hard for me to separate that out. And, finally, when we did settle in one neighborhood, that's when I really began feeling like, yes, this is a home. We were closer to being a family at that point.

Q. So, in general, you think that the self-concept a person has, his feelings about himself as a worthwhile person, may or may not have anything to do with adoption?

A.   Well, I think it can have a great deal to do with it. I've seen other children who in these instances were not told until very late in life, and it really undermined everything that they thought about themselves and their parents. For me, being told at the very beginning, it was just a given. And the attitude was: This is the way we live, this is what we live with and that's the way it is. So, in that instance, I think it's something you accept, like the color of your hair and the color of your eyes. You grow with it. You grow up with the idea that you are adopted.

Q.   I take it that you are talking about infant adoption, and I'm assuming that you were adopted when you were an infant.

A.   Yes.

Q.   You may know that there is some controversy going on right now about the word "chosen." What, from your point of view, do you think is desirable? Do you think the word "chosen" carries with it some implicit messages and what effect do you think this has on the child?

A.   It was used with me, and it was recommended, I believe at the time, by whoever was involved with my parents. It was used in the form that "we were able to choose you." It made me feel very special.

Q.   That anything you did was okay? Is that what you mean?

A.   Yes, but my parents were tempering that with me.

Q.   You knew that there were limits?

A.   Oh, yes.

Q.   And you knew what those limits were?

A.   But I think it can be used in a number of ways, some of which turn out to be to the child's detriment. I don't think that was the case with me, but it might have been. I do remember asking myself or wondering why I was so special and chosen. I still knew that there were definite boundaries. I was never allowed to behave just in any way I wanted to, but I also knew I was a special thing to them and they had chosen me in every sense of the word.

Q.   In one sense. In another sense, somebody chose you for them. They weren't the ones who did the choosing.

A.   Well, now, that's interesting. They told me that when they were allowed to go into the nursery and look at all the children and when my dad-to-be picked me up, I pulled on his tie; so, there was much more of a choosing process connected with this.

Q. I see. There were several infants around?
A. Now, that's what I'm not understanding. Whether somebody actually handed me to them or whether they could see others, I'm not really sure. I never clarified that. I remember the story being told several times, and I never pinned them down exactly as to whether there were three or four or five other infants crawling around. I don't know how it really happened, but the way it was told to me, in a way, was that I chose my parents by pulling on the tie. Maybe it's gotten more rosy in their memories as the years have gone by.

Q. Perhaps this is a good example to the "blue ribbon" concept baby. Because infant adoption in those days was considerably easier, it was only the most fit of all the children who were the survivors, in a sense. Those were also the days of delayed placement, I take it?
A. Yes, I was almost six months old when my parents adopted me. So, they missed a whole lot of my real early development; and, so, they tried to share with me all of the things they could remember from the time they had me.

Q. But really, in truth, the word "wanted" is more to the point, and I think that's what, really, a lot of people have in mind when they react to the business of being "chosen." For instance, in a family where there are both adopted children and biological children the word "chosen" would not be most appropriate term to use. What would this mean in terms of the biological children? So maybe the word "wanted" is more appropriate and, certainly, "wanted" is implied in the word "chosen."

Any fantasies that you can share with me about your birth parents?
A. I'm not sure these are fantasies or just thoughts, but my parents said that my original mother did wear glasses. I guess I would like to believe that she was fairly intelligent, had fair coloring like my own, and I guess I would like to believe that she really wanted me but just couldn't handle the responsibility. I always think of her as an older woman.

Q. Older?

A. Yes, maybe 30 to 35. Never as a young woman.

Q. Was she explained to you that way?

A. No. There was no age mentioned, no reference as to whether she was a teenager or in her 20's. I just always think that way; maybe because my own mother was in her 30's by the time I was adopted. Other than that, I really can't remember, but once in a while I do wonder what she might have looked like.

Q. How about the birth father?

A. I have an image of him too, and I think, for some reason, and maybe it's because of my own close association with my adoptive dad, who I consider my dad, that I might like to meet him. I don't know why not my original mother, but for some reason I have an inkling that someday maybe I will meet him. But I don't know what I would say if I did meet him.

Q. This is interesting, because I think the fantasy most of us have is that the birth father is viewed strictly as a necessary, but relatively unimportant, partner.

A. For some reason, I don't think of him as totally uninvolved. My fantasy is that there was a close relationship. Whether or not it might have led to marriage is something I often wonder about.

Q. Is there a sense of loss that occurs somewhere along the line?

A. I'm not sure, consciously, but just from what I understand of my own behavior, which is hard to be objective about, I can say this: Friends mean a lot to me, and people mean a lot to me. And death is very significant to me, like I really feel it. Whether that is a carry-over from a previous sense of loss or not, I don't know. I do know that I am so tuned in to the possibility of losing people, so much that sometimes I don't allow myself to get too close to them if I know they're going to be gone fairly soon. But as far as any other symptom, like grieving, I cannot say.

Q. Is adolescence harder for an adoptee?

A. I think so, a little. I don't know about male adoptees, but I have struggled with the question, "Do I tell my boyfriends or don't I?" especially if I've been dating them for a while and especially if the relationship may lead to marriage. When do I tell them is the question, and I believe I came to understand how my mother must have felt not to be able to have children. I was able to sympathize with her. Also, you are recognizing how children came into the world at that time of development, so it opens up that whole area of sexuality and childbearing.

Q. Did the term "illegitimacy" bother you?

A. Yes, because I didn't know about my own beginnings and I felt people made judgments about me because of the circumstances into which I was born, and I didn't think that was right. Yes, it does bother me, although not to the extent that it once did.

Q. Well, it would seem to me that if you're pretty clear on who you are this should not be that troublesome an issue. If you know who you are, then, it would appear that you get your sense of who you are in relation to the clarity of the communication from your parents that you are one of them.

A. Yes, and this became important with the extended family, and I was never singled out as "our adopted daughter" or "granddaughter." So, how the extended family deals with the adoption issue is very important.

Q. As you know, there is a controversy over the sealed record of the child's birth. Does that do anything to you? You know, the business of a conflict of rights between the adoptee, the birth parents and the adoptive parents?

A. I've done some research of my own on that question, and I don't have one set answer. That's why I don't think there can be one set policy to govern all situations. I wish, ideally, every case could be looked at on its own merits and on a case-by-case basis. I realize there may be overwhelming needs on the part of the adoptee to find out, but I don't feel that people who don't want to be contacted or disturbed should have these wishes violated. One of the suggestions is a mediating board which can act as a screening device for both the adoptee and the birth parent. If both independently desire a contact, a mediating board can be the means for such a meeting. That sounds great, but if it were a situation in which I were contacted by a board and told that one of my birth parents wanted to see me, then I would have to play the "heavy" and say "no." That would be an awful infringement. In practice, it is a very difficult situation to set out a uniform policy that works to everyone's satisfaction in all cases.

Q. Well, it is an awfully perplexing problem, to be sure, and I'm not sure there is any way to reconcile the conflicting rights of all parties concerned, because one of the givens at the time of the adoption is that this was a final decision, irrevocable, and that no biological parent went into this contract thinking that sometime in the future he or she would be approached by someone who said, "I know who you are." It is viewed as a final step, a break with the past, and having made this decision, he or she is in a position to put the pieces of his or her life back together and resume, as much as possible, a normal life.

A.   I agree, totally, and it's also a break for the adoptive parents.

Q.   Do you think adoptees have a greater sense of gratitude to their parents than non-adoptees?

A.   Yes.

Q.   Do you?

A.   I really do, and, for a while, I thought it was a problem for me and my marriage, because I am so devoted to my parents. Of course, being an only child doesn't aid that any, but that's why I leveled with my husband before I married him. I said, "This is the way it is." The pull is definitely there. I know they gave me a lot, but then I look at my husband and I know his parents gave him a lot, too. So, in retrospect, I'm not really sure I can answer that question in any definitive manner.

Q.   I can understand that because one can speak only from his or her standpoint. An adoptee cannot really state what his feelings for his parents might be if he were a biological child, and a biological child cannot really know what his feelings might be if he or she were adopted.

A.   I suppose you can say that they are responsible for a lot of what I am; but my looks, anything that is hereditary, they weren't responsible for. The whole nature-nurture question is one that fascinates me. While I like to give my adoptive parents all the credit, there are parts of me that are attributable to my genes.

Q.   Well, I happen to know you are quite gifted and, so, while you came with something, they nurtured it.

A.   Definitely, and in a different environment, it might not have been.

Q.   One final question: Is there something you think adoptive parents ought to know in rearing a child they adopted?

A.   They really have an opportunity to explore a different avenue in life and that it can be as rewarding an experience as natural parenthood. It's still parenting, and that is what is important, in spite of the differences. It is still the relationship that is the key. As far as certain pointers are concerned, I would stress honesty—total and complete in all things—and especially with an adopted child.

One concluding remark on special considerations during adolescence. Because adolescents are so sensitive to mixed messages, insincerity and hypocrisy, it is vital that adoptive parents get in touch with their own feelings first—before attempting to reassure their child about his own origins. Whether morally defensible or not, it is a common practice among adoptive parents to speak of the biological parents as "good people", having come from a highly respectable family, who because of age and general immaturity, gave the child up for adoption, putting the needs of the child over their own. This not only provides the child with a respectable pedigree, it allows the parents to gear their expectations to the highest level, and in addition, it feeds right into the family romance fantasy.

The danger is that when the story is essentially false, the adolescent knows it (because the nuances of the lie are so perceptible) and the relationship between parents and child is irreparably damaged rather than strengthened. The admonition "know thyself" is ever so true for adolescents.

This particular adoptee articulated some feelings about the adoptive experience for her. There was also a concern about her life prior to the time she was "chosen" by her parents; i.e., the first six months of her life. An interview with another adoptee answered some of the same questions in a similar way but at the same time, reflected a different point of view.

Q. Did you have an emotional reaction to the idea of being adopted?
A. In a way I did. I remember dealing with the question of illegitimacy and the idea of someone having given me up. It came across as rejection, which I think every adoptee deals with at some point of his/her life. I don't see how anyone who is adopted would not feel some pain or anger over that experience at some point. But at the same time, it was a kind of fleeting thing—it came and went, and I hardly ever think about it now.

Q. Has there been a sense of loss for you?
A. No. I only experienced the sense of gain. Its kind of hard to explain, but you cannot feel the loss of something that you don't know what it is. You have an image of people out there, but they don't have faces, they don't have features, so its hard to feel a loss of something you can't really visualize?

Q. Is there a sense of obligation toward your birth parents?
A. I feel I owed them gratitude for offering me a chance for the life and lifestyle I've led. Without them giving me up, I might not have had the type of life I've had with two loving parents who provided me with affection and satisfaction. For that I am very grateful.

Q. Is there a sense of obligation toward your adoptive parents?
A. I love my parents dearly. I know they made a conscious decision to have me because they could have gone through their life without children. But I'm not so sure that my sense of obligation is any greater than if they had been my biological parents.

Another adolescent adoptee objected to the societal bias he experienced over the years of his life insofar as his adoptive status is concerned.

Q. Looking back at the adoption experience, do you think people generally make too much of adoption?
A. I do, and I can't understand it. I know a lot of people who are adopted, I have a sister who is adopted and some friends who are (adopted), but I guess most people aren't. I don't understand what the big deal is.

Q. Have you heard the term "real parents" and do you have a reaction to it?
A. I have heard it lots of times and, frankly, it bothers me. To me, a "real parent" is one that hangs around and helps you grow up. I think it ironic that people use the word "real" because, in fact, these people, whoever they are, are very *unreal* to me.

Q. Can you talk a little more about how it bothers you?
A. When people say "you don't look like either of your parents," I jokingly say, "that's good news." But on the inside, it bothers me. Of course, there are many similarities between myself and

my parents and I find myself thinking the same way as my (adoptive) father does. So it rubs off.

Q. Do you have any special thoughts about being an adopted child?

A. At times I have thought of what kind of life I would have had if I were adopted into a different family. I could have been beaten or treated worse than if I had been kept by my birth parents.

Q. Does that thought bother you?

A. Yes.

Q. But you could have gone into a better home, actually, maybe one that would have given you a Ferrari.

A. Well, if you're spoiled and not given any love, its no use. But given that, I wouldn't mind having a Ferrari.

Q. Are birthdays special in terms of adoption? Do you think about your birth mother on those occasions?

A. No. As long as I can remember, its just been my (adoptive) mother and father. I don't think back.

Q. Many adoptive parents would be interested in knowing whether you have ever thought of a search. Can you comment on this?

A. I have thought about it but I'm really not interested in pursuing that. About the only reason why I would ever want to search would be to see what they look like, but that's not all that important, actually.

Q. Do you have any special pointers or instructions to adoptive parents on how to rear their children?

A. About the only thing I can think of is not to treat them any differently than if you have a child yourselves. This excludes age differences, of course. If you do treat them differently, they will use that against you and you won't have a very happy family.

The position stated by these young people is remarkably compatible with the basic thrust of this book: where children grow up feeling a part of the family, closely identified with them, and have received unconditional love from their parents, whatever conflicts arise in life, including identity issues, can be resolved with very little difficulty. On the other hand, in families where turmoil and family abuse reign supreme, verbal or otherwise, the situation is ripe for the heightening of identity conflicts, parent-child relationship difficulties, and poor self-esteem.

CHAPTER 9

RIGHT TO KNOW:
"ADOPTEES IN SEARCH"

A dopted children are an inseparable part of the adopted family and share in the heritage of that family. However, in the past several years, there has been a renewed interest in genealogy and the tracing of one's genetic "roots." This has impacted on many adopted children and reinforced desires they might have had to find their biological parents. There are some psychological bases for this search which will be discussed later, but at the outset let us consider the legal ramifications of this issue. First, under most state laws, all files, records, adoption processes are of a confidential nature and are open to inspection only under court order following a showing of a "good cause" or "compelling need" for such inspection. Those items included in this kind of provision are agency records, court proceedings, adoption petitions, original birth certificates, and court decrees. Although these laws govern the availability of all types of information relating to the biological background of an adoptee, adoption agencies and private placement intermediaries do, in fact, supply medical and other non-identifying information to adoptive parents at the time of adoption. This procedure is unofficially recognized as permissible for the courts even though the practice may be technically in violation of many statutes. However, this informal means of basic information retrieval is not available to adoptees with respect to information about their birth parents. Names and any identifying information (address, occupation and even physical descriptions) are strictly guarded by the intermediaries. Herein lies the controversy of the sealed adoption record—some adolescent and adult adoptees are currently seeking not only information about relinquishment, medical history, and circumstances of birth, but are requesting the names and addresses of birth parents for purposes of initiating contact and arranging meetings.

As to the law, there are several principles involved here. Despite arguments to the contrary, there is no Constitutional "right to know." The adoptee who searches for or wants to search for his or her biological roots has no Constitutional right to discover them. At the same time, the biological mother has no right to be protected from later intrusion—no right to privacy. These and other questions have been argued repeatedly throughout the country; and, uniformly, without exception, no court has given any constitutional sanction to these questions. The law of adoption is dictated purely by state laws. The sealed records laws are based upon a "privacy theory," not upon rights derived from our Constitution and Bill of Rights.

There are a number of people involved in the consideration of the issue of the "right to know." Obviously, one is the biological parent. When the consents are signed at the threshold of the adoption proceeding, the biological parent has a "right" to his or her (usually her) privacy. Notwithstanding the lack of a constitutional right to privacy (alluded to in the previous paragraph), she should be able to, as a matter of practice, heal her emotional scars, go about the business of "getting on" with her life, and not have to fear a very uncomfortable situation resurfacing in the future. She should be able to retain this privacy even if the laws were to change later, allowing the records to be opened, because at the time she signed the relinquishment papers, her understanding, the foundation of her contract, was to retain this privacy.

The second party in this process is the adoptive parent or parents. They have every right to have that child be their "own," without interference or undue worry. They are not taking this child on "lease." This child is going to be part and parcel of their family, from "Who is "Grandma and Grandpa?" to "Who is the 'black sheep' in the family (tree)?" The adoptive parents have every right to consider the child their own, without strings, without reservations, and without the ultimate worry in the back of their mind that somebody is going to make an emotional claim, if not a legal one, to their child. It is disturbing, or could be disturbing, to the adoptive parents and disruptive of the parent-child relationship.

The third party in this controversy is the child. The child should have the same type of consideration. Children face enough difficult developmental tasks as they grow up without adding unnecessary confusion. "Who are my 'real parents'?" should not be an issue. The child should have security in his relationship with his adoptive family and not have to unduly struggle with divided loyalties.

In addition to the birth parent(s), the adoptive parent(s), and the child, there is a fourth element involved, and that is the governmental entity. It has an interest in being part of the adoption, insuring that the adoption works and that there is a guarantee of security for all parties involved. The State also has an interest in the stability of the family, the child and the parents, in this whole process. However, there is a push in society to change the laws to offer more access to adoption records, and the government will have to respond accordingly.

What records are we talking about, though? Where can children go to get the information they desire?

First, an adoption is handled either by a agency or privately. That is probably the most fertile source of information. There are few laws in this country which restrict the distribution of this information from an agency or private source. If there is a lawyer, as a matter of ethics, the attorney cannot divulge what is in his files. The agency, whether public or private, as a matter of its own rules, might not be able to divulge information either, but the searchers might have the ability to bring a lawsuit to get that information because there are few specifics in the law on privacy involving the agency or the lawyer other than the construction already identified.

A second source of information is the court. The court file contains a report from an agency and includes consents. It contains the legal pleadings, and other information. It probably will not be as thorough as the information from an agency or private source, but there will be some information there. Most of those court records are sealed and cannot be opened without a showing of "good cause."

The third place for a search for records is the repository of the birth records, wherever that may be, (the registrar of the board of health), and those records are also sealed. There are three states where an adult adoptee over the age of twenty-one can get the original birth certificate—Alabama, Kansas and Alaska. All that source will do, though, is yield the name and possibly a birthplace. However, in these three states, if one is an adult adoptee, s/he can receive that information without a court order. In all the other states, in order to get a birth certificate, a court order is required—again, upon a showing of "good cause."

How does the law define "good cause?" Let us examine three separate hypothetical situations. First, let us suppose that an attorney makes a plea to the judge, saying, "My clients have a child who is adopted, and the child needs tissue typing done with biological family members in order to locate a kidney donor because he needs a transplant." This situation can be easily handled without divulging identities. Anonymity can be preserved while the request is met. That certainly is "good cause." Reasonable people could hardly differ on that. A second situation involves one with psychological ramifications. The lawyer states, "I have a situation where the young person is really confused, with terrible identification problems. He wakes up in the morning wondering who he really is." Several psychiatrists testify that this child must find his biological family to satisfy this need for identity. That also is probably a good case and shows "good cause." The third case presented involves an attorney who states, "Judge, I represent this young person. She is twenty-one years old and she would like to find her 'real mother' to satisfy her curiosity." The client will probably not win that case because that is probably not "good cause." The first two cases show real need—a medical problem and a psychological problem. However, the third illustration does not.

This is how the issue is currently being dealt with by the courts, on a case-by-case basis. In the last analysis, the judge is the ultimate arbitrator. Hopefully, the judge has a good sense of justice and sensitivity. There are some questions which a judge should ask in order to test "good cause" or "compelling need," which is the other legal phrase used in the statutes. They are:

1. Is the adoptee sincere?
2. Is the quest for information necessary for the adoptee's well being?
3. Will the adoptee refrain from using the information in a disadvantageous manner to himself or others?
4. Has there been any interference with the adoptee's work, school or personal life because of the desire to know?
5. Has consent been obtained from either or both of the biological parents?
6. Has consent been obtained from either or both adoptive parents?

A "no" answer to any one of these raises serious doubts as to whether or not "good cause" has been demonstrated and therefore, as to whether a judge will allow a disclosure.

There is one other area to consider and that concerns genealogists. What happens if they want to search records, and the issue at hand is great-grandma's adoption? This is a circumstance in which a search doesn't interfere with a family's privacy. There is no issue of sensitivity, because it does not affect the lives of living people. It is possible to make a good argument in court for the release of that kind of information which goes back several generations.

As has been reported in the media and literature, there is much strong feeling on both sides of the "sealed records controversy." Some states are currently considering legislation on this subject. It is hard to predict how many people would actually be affected by these laws. Statistics from countries which have open records—Scotland, the Scandinavian countries, Israel, and the Canadian province of Ontario—show two sets of disparate figures. The first set is for people who are told from the time they are very young that they are adopted. Those statistics indicate only one in 100 persons seeks out information about birth parents—even though in those countries all one has to do is state his/her name and age and request the records. However, statistics in these countries also show that people who are not told until the pre-teen or later of their status of adoptee have a much greater curiosity—40 in 100 or 4 in 10 seek information about their birth parents.

There are several probable reasons for this great statistical difference. One, if the adoptive parents don't tell the child about the adoptive status, it might indicate the adoptive parents' discomfort with the adoption process itself. Children are typically very perceptive about non-verbal as well as verbal cues demonstrating parental discomfort and anxiety, and it probably would affect his/her perceptions and feelings about the adoption when learned. Secondly, a delay in telling the child about the adoptive status has implications relating to parental honesty. The child may feel that the fact that the parents withheld such fundamental information for so long may suggest that they have withheld other vital information as well. This affects the child's relationship with his parents in a profound way, with disastrous consequences.

It is not possible to say how many people would be affected if the sealed record laws are changed. Obviously these are perplexing questions posed to all members of the adoption triangle. The purpose of inclusion in this chapter was to present the legal side. A subsequent chapter, (chapter 12), however, addresses the question more fully, including the findings of an important research study.

CHAPTER 10

THE BIRTH PARENTS

It is neither unusual nor atypical for adopters to wonder about the birth parents of their children. Questions surface in the adoptive parents' minds along the following lines. How did they decide on adoption? How do they feel about their decision? Was professional help available to them? If so, was it worthwhile? It is normal for parents to entertain fantasies about the birth parents, particularly the woman. The fact of the matter is that without the birth parents, there would be no institution of adoption. That is why we feel compelled to include a chapter on the subject in this book, just as we did in our previous work.

In contrast to the birth mother, we know virtually nothing about the birth father. About all we know is that he tends to be the same age, social class, and educational level as his pregnant girlfriend, that they have known each other for some time prior the conception, and that relationships between the pair are much more meaningful than previously presumed (Pannor, et. al., 1971).

Explanations of causes of unmarried parenthood derive largely from a psychological perspective. The social work profession, already committed to an application of psychoanalytic principles in its helping methods, tended to look less at social forces. Typical of such an outlook, Young (1954) describes the unmarried father in the following way:

> He is in almost every case a counterpart of the neurotic personality of the unmarried mother. Their problems complement each other with precision, and unconsciously each has sought in the other an answer to his own neurotic needs (p. 134)

Such explanations of unmarried parenthood were quite popular in the 1940's and 1950's and, despite the clinical and empirical support for such a position, there is a danger in attempting to identify a single cause theory addressing this problem. It is our view that multiple factors are prevalent with equally credible explanatory power. Today's teen culture is considerably more permissive about sexual activity and experimentation, which may have little, if anything, to do with unconscious motivations to produce a child. In this view, the pregnancy is, quite simply, an unintended consequence of sexual intercourse.

However correct or incorrect this impression happens to be (and there is not sufficient data to support a claim either way), the fact of the matter is that the field is fairly ignorant about the cause of unmarried fatherhood. For one thing, he may not even know that he is to become a father out of the need of many, if not most, unmarried mothers to virtually deny his existence.

There is an additional reason for this ignorance. Even if the agency were to contact him, an almost impenetrable barrier or moral condemnation frequently greets him. His own guilt feelings lead him to anticipate punishment; and all too often he receives just that—both from our laws and our punitive attitudes. The societal attitude that he is immoral, irresponsible, or just plain bad makes it improbable, if not impossible, to make meaningful contact with him.

This societal attitude reflects itself in a strange quirk in the literature. The adjective "putative" is frequently, if not invariably, used in referring to the birth father. This is really a derogatory reference aimed at the unmarried mother, for it means that he is the suspected, alleged or reputed father of the baby, suggesting a degree of promiscuity on her part. But in our experience, the vast majority of unmarried mothers are quite aware of the identity of the baby's father. And in light of *Stanley v. Illinois*, it is absolutely essential to identify him and apprise him of the forthcoming legal procedures relative to adoption.*

By contrast, there is a great deal of information concerning the mother. Most authors agree that she is not a stereotype but rather a human being who has been affected by a complex web of dynamics and circumstances, that the only thing they have in common is the carrying of the baby, and that the pregnancy is

---

*It is also interesting to note that in the isolated cases of biological fathers who desire to have the child placed with him, the procedures involved approximate those for an adoptive placement.

an obvious symptom of disturbed family relationships. Nevertheless, social agencies have viewed the unmarried mother's situation, based on their clinical experience, in a variety of stereotypical ways. The pregnancy was viewed as an attempted solution to personal or emotional problems. In some cases, the girl's pregnancy was seen as motivated by an unconscious wish to punish parents for being ungiving and unresponsive to her own needs. In still other cases, the pregnancy was viewed as an attempt to repair a precarious relationship with her own parents, particularly the mother, by creating a crisis around which the entire family can rally. Stereotypically, she is neither promiscuous nor unfeeling, but does have unresolved personal problems. As in the case of unmarried fathers, a minimizing of social forces and factors is quite prevalent.

Crisis theory allows us to understand the emotional trauma the young woman feels in dealing with her dilemma. The mechanism of denial may be pervasive and work for awhile, but prolonged cessation of menses, body changes and, finally, fetal movement makes her realize the full extent of her problem situation. While in some cases the denial extends throughout the entire pregnancy, this is indeed the rarest of cases. By the fifth month, she typically has to confront the reality of the situation, as denial no longer works, and anger over the pregnancy may take its place. She may experience loneliness, despair, and total abandonment. Telling the parents of her plight is one of the most difficult tasks facing her. By the time she comes to see a counselor, a depressive reaction may have set in.

The timeliness of treatment measures offered is another aspect of the process derived from crisis theory. Because the unmarried mother comes for help in a state of crisis and panic that has been precipitated by her pregnancy, she is particularly amenable to measures offered. (Of course, exacerbating elements of her own mother's anxiety, her father's withdrawal and her boyfriend's emotional and physical isolation only serve to heighten her own sense of hopelessness.) Studies indicate that the more timely the help proffered, the more immediate and efficacious the results. It is, therefore, vital that the physician recognize the signs of loneliness and despair and be attuned to her psychological needs. While it is undoubtedly easier for the woman to undergo a physical examination, counseling should be considered from the outset. Again, it has been our experience that those who have availed themselves of counseling measures offered, and who have dealt with the loss and betrayal issues paramount in the uniqueness of these problems, are the same women who are finally able to "let go" and resume their lives postpartally.

On the other hand, many unmarried mothers choose to forego counseling measures for a variety of reasons. For some, the denial may still be operative, at least regarding their feelings about the anticipatory loss. Such a girl told us "I just want to get this over with once and for all. I don't want to see the baby, know if it's well, or what sex it is. I just want to be knocked out throughout the delivery and pretend it never happened so that I can go on with my life." Another reason for rejecting counseling is because the thought of loss is too painful, emotionally—by not talking about their feelings, the sense of loss is somehow dissipated, or repressed.

The literature on working with the unmarried mother is couched in an assumption that she will essentially give the baby up for adoption, and that she has a right to anticipate some happiness in life regardless of the difficulty in which she finds herself. While giving the baby up for adoption is still an option available to her, the current atmosphere of increased acceptance of single parent motherhood has presented her with the viable alternative of keeping the child and rearing it herself, or allowing her own mother to help in the day-to-day care. In light of this, the advice given is as follows:

> "I will help you arrive at a decision regarding the care of the baby by helping you think through just what it is you wish to do. I will not advise you what to do but will help you think through the consequences or effects of any decision under consideration."

The neutrality of the worker's position cannot be overemphasized. Because messages can be so subtlely and unconsciously communicated, the worker must know and control his/her own predilection or biases. For both ethical and legal reasons, the girl must be truly free to make the decision regarding placement and consider what it is that she wishes to do. This is not to state that the worker cannot entertain a personal or clinical opinion regarding the best interest of the child but must keep it under control. To do otherwise might unethically influence her judgement and might even be in violation of the "informed consent", thereby jeopardizing the validity of the entire adoption process.

There are a number of psychological mechanisms used by the girl to protect herself from the overwhelming feelings of attachment and loss. One of these is rationalization. She tells herself that without her pregnancy, an infertile couple would not have the experience of parenthood. A variation of this theme is that giving up the baby is the decent thing to do, a charitable act of the highest order, and that out of an expression of love for the child, a double grace, as it were, is accomplished; providing a two-parent home for a child and providing a baby for a childless couple. Still another variant (of this same theme), particularly for girls with a religious or spiritual bent, is the thinking that she is, in a sense, God's instrument for the aforementioned double grace. What makes all of these examples a rationalization is that there is a current of reality in their thinking. Another mechanism used to defend herself from the pain of loss is thinking about the baby, not as her own baby, but as the adoptive couple's baby. This is, essentially, the defense of isolation, wherein the thought is emotionally disconnected from the feeling associated with that thought.

During the critical stages of working through the feelings of anguish, loneliness, fear and panic, she will frequently encounter disturbing thoughts of one kind or another. Some thoughts about parenting the baby are frightening when she considers that awesome responsibility associated therewith. Some thoughts about placing the baby are associated with guilt feelings relative to this decision. In our experience there is no one set pattern. Literally weeks go by during which time she is absolutely convinced that her decision—whatever it is—is the correct decision for her. In subsequent weeks, the opposite decision will evoke the same reaction of certainty. What is important to remember is that such vacillation is quite common and crucial to the decision-making process. We refer to such vacillation as "head—heart" responses. The head response is basically an intellectual one. It says: "I am pregnant. I am not in a position to give this child a home and the love he needs and he is better off placed with a family that can provide him with the love and security he needs." This response is tied to the decision to place, obviously. The heart response is emotional and linked to the decision to keep. It goes as follows: "This is my baby. I have a bond with it, we live off each other and need each other. Nobody has a greater right to this baby than the natural mother, and I am that person." Until the heart and head responses find some means of accommodating each other, confusion reigns for awhile, but is dissipated through a supportive therapeutic relationship.

The task of counseling is twofold:

1. Assisting the girl in bringing the range of her feelings out in the open, and
2. Helping her in making a decison with which she can live for life, taking into account her feelings toward herself, the baby, the birth father, and her own family.

Her feelings often revolve around concern for the baby and its future, her belief that she has betrayed her parents' trust in her, fantasies about the child's perception of her decision and anger over the circumstances which precipitated her need to make such a difficult and painful decision.

Feelings of the birth mother during this time (of pregnancy) are dependent on a number of factors: attitudes of her own parents; i.e., the extent to which the girl feels they truly understand and are supportive, the attitudes of the birth father, her age and level of maturity, and the extent to which she is able to distance herself, emotionally, from the biological bond that is occuring within her. There are three specific types of feelings we have noted, though they may be more or less of a variant nature, depending on the uniqueness of the circumstances. The first of these is guilt. While she may attempt to rationalize her decision to place the baby for adoption, an underlying feeling of guilt is related to the perception of abandoning her responsibility to the baby. Guilt may also be stirred up in some girls for wishing to keep the baby because, by her decision, the child is being deprived of a waiting, loving, two-parent situation. The second of these feelings is anger—about being in this predicament (the "why me?" response), and the perception, rightly or wrongly, that other people are interested in her only because she has something they want (the baby). Consideration of her as a human being, with wants and needs of her own, are not at all evident to her. The third feeling is an overwhelming sense of loss, particularly if adoption placement is the considered plan. Many young women who leave the hospital experience a grief reaction akin to the death of a child. Almost invariably, the sight of a newborn will elicit a totally unexpected crying spell. At this point, everyone is aware that she is finally in touch with her feelings (of loss).

A warm, supportive, nonjudgmental atmosphere will allow the woman to think through her situation and discuss the practical aspects of her planning free from coercion. The counselor who helps the unmarried woman face the thunderous impact of losing a child is responsible for helping her examine her own life as well as the life of her unborn child. This may involve assistance with housing or employment, but most importantly, involves helping her to identify her strengths and, as she finds satisfaction in making the decision best for herself and the baby, helping her to feel good about herself.

In assisting the woman in decision-making, the counselor must help her to separate fact from fantasy, help her to see the realities involved with raising a child alone and with relinquishing a child she may never see again. Although not always successful in this respect, the counselor who genuinely respects the woman and offers sincere help and understanding during this painful time in her life will become an important support system for the woman.

There have been very few systematic attempts to evaluate the overall effects of the pregnancy and consequent decision-making for the unmarried woman. Evidence is increasingly clear, however, that the unmarried mother feels she is completely alone in an insensitive, uncaring world. Recent research recognizes that even prior to relinquishing the child, perhaps as soon as she first experiences fetal movement, she experiences a grief reaction in anticipation of the loss. The denial of pregnancy, which can be equated with the denial stage characteristic of all mourning reactions, may be experienced in conjunction with the feeling of fetal movement, leading to intensely conflicting emotions.

As the delivery date approaches, the anxiety mounts accordingly. The co-existing emotions of attachment and detachment are confusing. Love for the baby, guilt over relinquishing her responsibilities, concern for the baby's future, and loss over what she thinks would be fulfilling experiences of observing the miracle of growth are obviously perceptions of considerable consternation for her.

The flood of emotions can erupt into fits of anger and rage. Usually the girl herself is unaware of her own dependency needs, her needs to be taken care of, and may verbally attack *anyone* with whom she comes into contact.

129

Renee was 17 years old, a high school junior with better than average grades, who learned of her pregnancy during the sixth month. Having been born as an illegitimate child herself, she had strong feelings about the poor care she received at the hands of her mother. In Renee's case, her own plans during the pregnancy were complicated by her mother's demand that Renee find another place to live. After consulting an attorney who agreed to place the baby, Renee was housed by a young couple (not the prospective adoptive parents) who agreed to board Renee as a charitable gesture.

Counseling measures were instituted as a precautionary measure to assure that all the services Renee might need would be available to her. During the first two sessions, Renee spoke openly about her view that a child needs a two-parent family, that she was unable to provide it with the nurturing needed, that a child needs more than mere material subsistence, and that she should have been placed herself by her mother rather than attempt to become a struggling single-parent family. (It became obvious to the counselor that Renee was viewing the unborn child as an extension of herself, and that she could make the decision she believed her mother ought to have made years ago.)

Just when everything seemed to be going according to schedule, Renee called the counselor to state that she wouldn't need to see him again. When asked why, she launched into a tirade about how she was feeling used throughout this entire process. She enumerated who was getting something out of her pregnancy: the adoptive parents; the doctor; the lawyer; and the counselor. All she was getting was the pain—both physical and psychological—and would have nothing to show for her investment.

At the hospital, Renee continued to exhibit the same pattern of behavior with the hospital social worker. At first she was congenial, expressing the view that she was comfortable with her decision to place the baby. But her irritation mounted with each question of exploring her feelings, and in a rage, ordered the social worker out of her room. She eventually signed the release but it was obvious to all that the only way in which Renee could surrender her rights to the baby was with dramatic and histrionic attack on people she was convinced were out to exploit her.

Expressions of anger are not uncommon in response to the range of emotions the young woman faces. A grieving period is necessary but one should remember that not everyone does her grief work in the same way. With some it is rather prolonged, lasting months or even years. With others, the mourning period virtually escapes detection. Of course, many grieve quietly because they were conditioned not to show feelings of hurt, shame, or embarrassment. The important thing to remember, though, is that whether the grieving takes a month or a year, it involves a process which cannot be dictated by the intellect or logical reasoning; it is dictated by the emotional makeup of the individual in question and how she typically and characteristically deals with separation and loss.

One young woman was surprised at her emotional reaction after placement, not realizing its thunderous impact on her. "My arms ache because I'll never be able to hold him. My overall feeling is that I feel cheated. I feel cheated because I won't be around to see him cut his first tooth. I feel cheated because I won't be there when he comes home from school. I feel cheated because I won't be there to see him go off to his prom . . . or to see him graduate from high school. I feel cheated because I won't be a part of his life when he gets married."

The decision to place or not to place is a mighty one, indeed, and for the first time, the unmarried mother must make the most momentous decision in her young life. Some girls panic and even want others to make that decision for her.

Pamela was 16 years old and had dropped out of her junior year in high school three weeks before the delivery date. After a normal labor and delivery, she scarcely looked at her newborn son. When she was asked what she wanted to do, she said that she knew she couldn't bring the baby home as her mother was ill and unable to care for the child. Pamela wanted to return to school the following semester. When asked about signing the consent, she balked and asked if the baby could be placed in a foster home while she sorted out her own feelings.

Visitation was irregular but even when she visited, the emotional distance she maintained with the baby was obvious to all. It was apparent that she was attempting to protect herself from any form of maternal attachment.

After four months of very little activity on the case, Pam was asked what her plans were in relation to the baby. She again balked, stating she needed more time. The social worker told her she could have no more than an additional two months, but that some decision would have to be made at that time. She agreed.

The additional two months went by with no visitation and no plan to take the baby home. The agency decided, at that point, that the decision was too weighty for Pamela to handle, and all of her actions seemed to indicate that she wanted the court to decide for her, and that she would abide by the involuntary termination as determined by the court.

This line of thinking was explained logically and carefully to the judge. However, he did not heed the advice of the agency worker, and put the question directly on Pam's shoulders. He said, in effect: "Pamela, this is your baby. Either you take him home or you surrender your rights to him. There is no other option." Pam looked at the surrender papers, her hand trembling, signed it, and bolted out of the courtroom, crying disconsolately. The court made her face her guilt about not wanting to assume this responsibility.

This case illustrates several points about the practice of termination of parental rights and adoption practice:

1. It is considered poor placement practice and, indeed, detrimental to a child's growth and development, to remain in foster care for an extended period of time. In all probability, the six month waiting period was too long, posing problems of bonding with the eventual adoptive parents.

2. Pamela's immaturity level was such that she could not accept the responsibility of making, in effect, an adult decision.

3. The courts have tended to view an involuntary termination with the gravest of reservations. Taking a legalistic position, the evidence would have to be quite weighty before such action would be deemed justifiable.

Not all birth mothers let go with the anger and struggle characterized by Renee and Pamela. Some let go with a rational, logical process, the thinking of which is revealed in the following interview.

Q. When you found out you were pregnant, what was your immediate reaction and what was some of your thinking?
A. I guess my first response was "why me?" Why couldn't it have been anybody else in the world but me? Then I started hoping, I guess, that somehow I was wrong, —that something else was causing this.

Q. Where about in this pregnancy was it that you knew —your first month?
A. Oh, I knew right away.

Q. You knew right away?
A. I knew after three weeks that I was pregnant. I went to a doctor when I was four and a half months along just to try to convince myself, I guess, that I was wrong.

Q. Well, when you said "why me," that didn't sound like a denial kind of response. It sounded like an anger response. The denial response would have been "not me." Did that come across too?
A. Yes, but I don't remember that one came before the other. They were all kind of bunched up together.

Q. When was it that you were able to tell people—like family?
A. Well, I didn't tell my family until when I went to the doctor, four and a half months later, so I could show them I got help from the doctor, and then I told my parents. And I told the rest of the family and most of my friends and most of my other relatives.

Q. Do you remember the reaction of your family?
A. They handled it a lot better than I thought they would; I would say it was very supportive.

Q. They were concerned about what you were going through. Is that right?
A. Right. In talking to me about my options and whether I have made a decision. I decided right away that I was going to place the child.

Q. Was there wavering in that decision?
A. Not really. In the hospital when I was holding the baby, I came, I guess, as close as I ever did in changing my mind.

Q. How long a period of time did you hold the baby?

A. I guess totally it was a few hours.

Q. That's holding it a long time.

A. I held the baby right after I had him, and then the next day I went to the nursery and held him and fed him his bottle, and I did that the next day, and the next morning I went home.

Q. How did they work out the actual legal part of it—in terms of the signing?

A. My caseworker came to the hospital the morning I was released and I signed the necessary papers.

Q. Was there any wavering at that point?

A. It was the most difficult point, but my mother was there, and I guess I was satisfied about my decision and knew I could not change it at this emotional period.

Q. While you were in the period of pregnancy thinking about the child going into an adoptive home, what were the thoughts that came to your mind about what sort of people would become the parents of the child? Were there any preconceived notions you had about what kind of life these people led or whether there was a match as far as religious affiliation and that sort of thing?

A. For the first seven months, I had planned on adoption and actually went to classes. I knew that the mother was a secretary to the lawyer handling the adoption. I knew at the time what the father did, but I don't remember now. But once I decided to go through the agency they gave me some information about the people. In fact, they gave me information about five different couples who were eligible and asked me if I had any preferences. They also told me that while they wouldn't guarantee my selection, they would give it strong consideration. At the time it seemed very important but now I don't remember any of it.

Q. So you actually had some say so in terms of who they were ultimately going to pick.

A. At the time I felt very, very strange as if I had some control over his future.

Q. How important was the religious matching?

A. Not a whole lot. I do know that a couple of families were Catholic. I told them it would be nice but it wasn't one of my priorities.

Q. Let's back up just a little bit to the pregnancy. Usually in my counseling young women who are in this situation, I ask the question "of all the problems you are having right now, what is the most difficult? What part about the whole thing bothered you the most?

A. One of the problems was the relationship with my mother. Looking back, I can see how hard she was trying to be supportive. Many times she was a big help, but at other times it was very difficult for me because we didn't talk enough and we did not always agree on what she wanted to do. I thought she was trying to hide the whole thing from all her relatives and her friends because she felt ashamed of me.

Q. You thought she was ashamed of you?
A. I thought she was.

Q. Oh, I see.
A. Now I don't think she was.

Q. Have you talked about this with her?
A. And she thought that I was feeling ashamed of myself and didn't want anyone to know. That was just a lack of communication.

Q. Which happens a lot.
A. I know.

Q. Some of the more typical responses I get to that question is an angry response. They say "why am I in this boat?" A lot of people think, well, not everybody gets pregnant, "why me, why am I being singled out? The other response I get a lot of is a feeling of betrayal of the trust that my parents have developed. Is there any of that?

A. I felt that way very, very strongly at first. The day after I told my parents my father took me out to lunch and brought the subject up deliberately, and told me that they did not feel betrayed,—that it could have happened to anybody and that I shouldn't feel ashamed. I did kind of feel like I had betrayed my mother, though. But it ended up that I really didn't. The hardest part was before I told my parents. I thought it would be probably be much more difficult once I told them, but it wasn't.

Q. So you went through a lot of mental anguish before you told them.

A. Yes.

Q. So maybe one of the best things was then to just get it out and tell them.
A. Right.

Q. Was your decision to place the baby hard for them?
A. Yes, in a way. I know that at the time when I signed the release papers it was really difficult for my mother. My parents wanted to see the baby.

Q. Was this their first grandchild?
A. No.

Q. No?
A. This was their second. But they were also very supportive of my decision and they agreed with me that they thought it was best.

Q. How about the year following the child going into an adoptive home? How was it?
A. The first few months were traumatic, I guess. As time went on it got to be very bad.

Q. I see.
A. Christmas was very difficult. His birthday the first year was also a hard time.

Q. You did a lot of crying on his first birthday?
A. Sure, I did a lot of crying for the first few months. Well, I kept a journal and one day I wrote: "Last night was the first time in ages I haven't cried myself to sleep," and that was a milestone, I guess.

Q. So, it is correct to interpret that to mean that you did a lot of thinking about him and how and what kind of experiences he was getting, was he being given enough care, and so forth, that sort of thing.
A. Yes, whether he was healthy was a big concern.

Q. Would you say, and this might be a very difficult question, but would you say that the sense of loss was great, moderate, mild, or not at all?
A. At first it was tremendous, but later on, the hurt and the sense of loss kind of faded—though not completely.

Q. How about counseling during this period of time? Were you given counseling in terms of what some of the emotional reactions might be?
A. I talked to my caseworker and she recommended there was a support group of girls who had placed children through that agency and I was going to go, but suddenly I decided I didn't want to because they started meeting right after I gave up the baby and, for me, it was too close.

Q. Did you ever go to them?
A. No.

Q. Have you dated a lot since this whole experience?
A. Not much. Who would want to trust in another relationship?

Q. I guess this is a way of protecting yourself from an experience like this.
A. Yes. That is definitely true. I think I'll be a lot slower in relationships in the future.

Q. Makes a lot of sense.

Q. I understand that you read our first book (*You're Our Child*) and commented that when you read the book, you felt it almost treated the birth mother as if she was part of a test tube experiment and the procedure did not really recognize her part in all this.
A. I guess what I felt when I first read it was that there was no recognition of the emotional factor involved in giving up your child.

Q. Not even under the chapter on birth mothers?
A. I think the first time I read it, no, but I have gone back and read it since. I think I was being overly critical, overly sensitive. But from the first reading, I got the impression that these adoptive parents don't realize what a warm, concerned person the birth mother is to give up a child because she can't provide a good home for him.

Q. It was never my intention to portray her as anything but that. As a matter of fact, the young woman who I used the transcript for, in that interview, it was clear that she was still struggling with feelings of loss. But I didn't want to make any interpretations. I knew that she was a sensitive person and knew that it was very obvious that she was concerned about the child and the care the child was getting. Her fantasies were that the child was receiving only positive things in his life and that any other kind of life was unthinkable.

A. I have that same fantasy. I guess my biggest fantasy about the child is that someday when he gets married and has kids of his own, he will come and find me and we will just have a talk, and he will be very accepting. I think my biggest fear is that he won't turn out as well and he will blame me for what went wrong in his life.

Q. What would be your response to anything else that comes up, if he knocks on your door and let's say you were already married and had two additional children and he says that: "I am the boy you gave up for adoption 21 years ago." What would your first response be?

A. My first response would be shock, I'm sure. I guess after that it would depend on how he feels about it. If he is angry and looking me up because he wants to rant and rave at me about what a terrible thing I did to him, then I would be crushed because my intentions were for nothing but the best for him and myself too. But, if he came just caring to see what I looked like, he would be very welcome. I would like to get to know him.

Q. You are 21 years-old. You are healthy and attractive. I see no reason why you would not married in the future. Have you given any thoughts to telling any prospective suitor, future husband, about this experience?

A. Yes, I think I would. But not until a meaningful relationship had developed.

Q. Do you believe in total honesty?

A. Yes, I want to tell my children as well. I don't know at what age. But I will tell them. I don't see any reason to hide it.

In an interview with a 16 year-old whose sense of loss is quite strong, we can see the myriad ways her thoughts about the baby continue to be expressed. Bev had a good relationship with her caseworker, who felt it important to maintain contact subsequent to the placement.

Q. Let me start out this way. A lot of adoptive parents, and I'm one too, have a lot of concern about the birth parent, particularly the mother, because she's the one we identify with most.

Some of the questions I'm going to ask you have to do with what the experience has been like for you after you delivered the baby. Since I do a lot of counseling with birth mothers I know that a lot or most of them have to deal with the whole decision-making process saying: "Gee, I'm in a difficult position, I've got to make a decision, and without a doubt it's the most difficult decision of my life, and one of the things that bothers me the most is that I'm going to develop these feelings of attachment to the baby and so how do I keep myself at some kind of distance and at the same time recognize that I do have these normal, maternal feelings." The sense of eventual loss, then, is that something that you had to think about?

A. When I decided to give the baby up for adoption, I didn't think that I loved the baby. I just wanted to throw it away, get rid of it, not worry about it, go on with my life. But once the baby was born I had to really say hey, this is a baby. There's a lot of love and I felt I loved it more than anything in the world. I felt a loss. It took a long time for me to get over it but I've gotten over it now and I know deep in my heart that I did do the right thing because there was no way I could raise her. I mean, I could give her lots of love but I'm not ready to be a mother yet and I know she's with somebody now that loves her to death and she's got everything her little heart desires. But I do feel a loss. I just keep hoping that someday maybe she'll come to me but I'll never go to her because I don't want to interrupt her life and if she doesn't want me in it, that's fine. She will know better than anybody else and she's got to be happy.

Q. One of the questions or one of the ways I put it when I counsel birth mothers is before they deliver, I talk about the head and heart reaction and the head reactions are the same sort of things that you were talking about. "I'm 16, 17, or I'm 20 and I'm not married and I'm not in the position to give the baby the kind of care and devotion she needs. Because mothering is more than just putting food on the table and there are people out there who really want a baby and who are able to give the baby the things she wants, so therefore the best decision I can make is to place the baby for adoption." That's what I call a head reaction. But then there's the other part, the heart reaction. The heart reaction says something like, "This baby is growing inside me, we are a unit, I have a real feelings for this baby, nobody has more

of a right to this baby than I do since we're living off of each other. Therefore, I don't see how I can separate from the baby and therefore I want to keep the baby."
A. I said that.

Q. So you went through those kinds of head and heart reactions?
A. Yes. I didn't go through that until the day I had to go down and sign the papers and that's when it really hit me. I was up all night thinking of anyway possible that I could keep her and everything would be alright. But, you know, my mom, she supported me the whole way telling me that whatever my decision, she would back me. But that I had better be realistic about what I could and could not do for the baby.

Q. Is there a concern that you have that as the years unfold about how the baby is going to think about you? What thoughts she's going to have about you, whether she's going to think well of you or whether she's going to be angry? Could you share some of those thoughts with me?
A. I hope she doesn't hate me for it. I wrote her a letter.

Q. You did?
A. Yes, and I explained to her why I did what I did and it's all in the letter, and her adoptive parents have agreed to give that to her when she's old enough to really understand.

Q. They've agreed to give it to her?
A. Yes. That's part of the policy where I put her up for adoption. She will know someday that she's adopted and that's part of the agency's thing. So she will know and I'm glad about that because I wouldn't want them to hide it from her. I know if I was adopted I would want to know. I wouldn't want to find that out when I was 20 years old. I would feel very betrayed. I'm glad she's going to know. I hope she doesn't hate me but if she does, then I really can't blame her. I mean, I did what I thought was right and I hope she thinks I did it for her own good because I did.

Q. Well, I'm sure that she'll think you did it for her own good but perhaps, and this is a head reaction, and there may be a feeling somewhere along, saying, "Up until now adoption has been great. People wanted it and I feel chosen but in order for this to have happened, somebody didn't want me and that hurts."
A. Well, it's not that I didn't want her. I wanted her and I would do anything in the world if I could have kept her.

Q. What you didn't want and didn't feel ready for was the responsibility.

Q. Do you know much about the adoptive family?
A. The people that adopted my baby have a son already and when they came in for the interview for this next adoption, they brought their son in and the caseworker had asked him something about adoption and he went up and said "I'm adopted." And she asked him, "well, what does that mean?" And he said "that means that I'm very special."

Q. When you talk about your baby, do you think of this as your baby or do you think of this as a baby who now belongs to such and such people?
A. I still think she's my baby. I may not be the person that's raising her but, you know, I made her come into this world and she's my baby. At the same time, I realize she is not only my baby but she's two other people's baby.

Q. It's a sharing kind of thing.
A. Yeah.

Q. Let's talk for a minute about the open adoption concept. When I first met you and heard you comment about the practice of visiting the child regularly, I heard you say something I had never heard from a birth mother before and that was that it would have been very difficult for you. If you had to do that, it would be a constant reminder of the pain that you went through in giving up the baby.
A. I couldn't do it that way because everytime I would see her I would want to take her home because I will always think of her as my baby and those feelings would come back again. You know, I gave birth to her, she's my baby and she should be with me, I don't think it's fair to the child. I've seen plenty of shows on TV of the birth parent trying to get the baby back after a number of years and I could never do that. I mean, I'm her mommy because I gave birth to her but I'm not her mommy, I'm not the one that gave her the care and that wouldn't be very fair to her. Like I said before, she's the innocent one. She doesn't deserve that and I know if I would see her I would probably be tempted to do it.

Q. The thing that I've never been able to figure out on this open adoption concept is from the child's point of view, and nobody

really knows the answer to this question. How would the child look at you and what is your role with that child?
A. She would just be confused.

Q. Adoptees I've talked to said that's very confusing and that's something that I have a hard time dealing with.
A. I'm glad I didn't go through open adoption. I could have. I guess when I went to Social Services, I had my choice on just about anything. Whatever way I wanted to do it was alright. They sure give the birth parents whatever they want these days.

Q. I get the impression in talking to you that this is not a closed chapter in your life, that there is a tremendous attachment to that baby, still.
A. Yeah there is, but I've accepted it.

Q. There again, that's the head response.
A. My heart would say go to her. If I let my heart rule me, it would say go get her back but then I think hey, I can't afford this.

Q. And that's the head reaction.
A. Yes, I suppose so.

Q. How deep was your sense of loss?
A. It was very great at first.

Q. When did you get that? A month anniversary?
A. Oh when I see...like when I'm in a bad mood or I'm depressed about something I just start thinking about it or if I see a little baby that's her age I really start thinking about it and just times when I feel real lonely and down I just start thinking about it and I get myself all worked up and all depressed and I just call my caseworker. I've got her home phone number and so when I get like that, I just call her.

Q. Sounds like a very special relationship that you have with her.
A. We got really close in the couple of months that I talked to her, really close. I'm very strong about adoption. At first, I always said that if I ever got pregnant, I was going to keep it, but then you know, I talked to her and one thing about her, she never told me I was wrong. She said whatever you decide, it's your life, you know, and since I talked to her, I think about it and I think adoption is the right thing.

Q. I just really have one more question and that has to do with your writing a letter to the baby. Could you share with me what you said in that letter or if the baby was sitting here right now, what would you be saying?

A. Well, in the letter I just told her the situation I was in because Tom and I were not together, we had broken up and right when the baby was born, he did not have a very good job and I didn't have any job. I told her that I thought she would be better off with someone that could take better care of her and I told her that she should not forget that I do love her and its not that I didn't want her but I just thought she would be better off. My caseworker told me that the adoptive parents were so happy that the mother cried, she was so happy. It makes me feel good to know that I made some people happy, you know. As long as my baby's happy that's all I care about. As long as they're good to her. They must be pretty good people if they've got one adopted child and they got another one, they must be pretty good people. It kind of makes me feel safer that this was their second. They've already passed the test once.

Q. So you trust that whatever happens to this baby are going to be good things.

A. Yeah. I mean I'm for adoption. I believe in it.

Q. Do you have feelings toward the adoptive parents since you don't know a lot about them?

A. I know they have a lot of responsibility. But I think they'll do a good job and if they weren't fit to be parents, they wouldn't be approved by the agency. I came from parents that are divorced and I feel strongly that a child needs two parents.

Q. Any final thoughts you would like to share?

A. I think adoptive parents have a right to know how we feel, and you know, we have feelings too, and we're giving a gift to them and it's a very special gift. I think they should know how we feel about giving them this gift.

A. I hope someday my little girl will come and find me because I would love to see her. I don't expect her to say "there's my mom" you know, I don't expect her to run up and say "mom," or anything like that but I hope I can be a good friend. I don't ever expect her to call me mom but as long as I could be a part of her life, that would be nice. I would like to think that I can be a part of her life.

The final interview is with 35 year-old Nancy, who requested the opportunity to talk about her feelings relative to the child she placed for adoption some 15 years ago.

Q.   What is it that you had in mind in wanting to come forward after all these years?
A.   Talking about it helps to get things in focus. You can sort it out better if you verbalize. It's been a long time since I made that decision and I thought I had it all neatly packaged and put away on the shelf somewhere. But in the last few years feelings have started to re-surface and maybe it's my age. I don't know why exactly, but I want to deal with it effectively and I thought maybe I can turn up something that seemed negative then into something positive for me by talking about it as a means of therapy and also to help other people who might be going through this as well. To be able to see and help someone who has to deal with it and is still dealing with it.

Q.   You said feelings have re-surfaced. You want to tell me what some of those feelings are?
A.   Maybe feelings of guilt, curiosity about the child, wondering sometimes if I did the right thing. I think deep down I know I did but I am that child's mother and I can't know that child, I can't know what kind of person she's become but I would like to and I guess I think now that all this time has gone by, making the decision that I had to make is not an easy one. But later on when you think about the baby growing into a person you think maybe you would like to know that person and have a chance to meet that person and explain personally as a mother why you did what you did to that child. I mean, I think that if I was an adopted child I would like to know and have a chance to meet my mother. As a girl, I would like to be able to see her and meet her and see what kind of person she is. And I would like to know myself from her why she did what she did. And it seems that would weigh on me after a while. And from the other end, I would like to be able to explain that personally and not have somebody else do my talking for me.

Q.   You would like to explain what reasons you had for giving her up, is that right?
A.   Yes, to let her know that it wasn't that she wasn't loved. I don't know if there would be anything alike between us if we ever

did meet but I would just like a chance to tell her, you know, face to face and from my point of view why I did what I did, so that she would know she was loved and it wasn't a matter of convenience. I was thinking about her best interests and loving her, which allowed me to make my decisions.

Q. So you're saying you placed her for adoption out of love, is that right?

A. Because I didn't feel that at that point and time I could be a good mother, I didn't know what the future would bring. I guess in some ways you could look at it as the easy way out but I didn't think so at the time. I think the easy way out was to keep her and go on.

Q. And you let her go because. . . .

A. There are a lot of reasons. I mean, it would have been hard to keep her and go on as a single parent. I knew that. That was part of it. There was pressure from parents who could not handle the situation. I knew I would be on my own. I mean, they would be supportive but you love your parents too, and at a time like that you are torn. There are a lot of reasons why I did what I did but I guess my survival mechanism is falling back on that I did it with her as the main focus. Throughout it all there was a lot of confusion, a lot of pressure, I was afraid, but I thought, "who is the innocent victim in all of this, the child." And how would she fare better, with a mother who would try to be both parents or give her a chance to have two parents who really want a child and can't have one of their own. They can love her and give her the type of love and security she needs. That's what carried me through, was keeping the child in focus. That's what helped me to make a decision.

Q. Well, now that you have talked about it, a certain sadness comes through and you get a feeling of loss.

A. Yes, I feel, I don't know about every mother, I can't speak for every mother, but that child is a part of me physically and maybe psychologically, I feel that there are ties that for me were never completely severed. And that's why they are re-surfacing I guess.

Q. What does it take to completely sever those ties, do you have any idea?

A. I don't think you can. Because it is not, you can't sign the paper and suddenly say I'm not going to think about that person again and I'm out of her life, this ends it. Legally you have given the child up for adoption but that doesn't stop the heartache that you feel sometimes.

Q. So you are talking about the signing as a very difficult thing psychologically and this pain doesn't go away. Does the pain lessen after time?
A. It sort of comes and goes.

Q. Is that right? Are there certain times of the year that. . . .
A. Holidays maybe, there might be a movie on TV or an article that you read that appears like a zoom lens, everything just comes zeroing in and you don't seem to have a lot of control over it. And then you deal with it right then and there and go on. It never goes away, not for me.

Q. Well I think that one part is the giving up the baby legally. Legally the child is no longer yours and legally, she belongs to some other people. But then it seems to me that there is something else here that goes with this and that is living with the knowledge that you did this and the stigma of a sense of shame that goes with it. That is, nobody must know this. I'm just asking if this is a problem.
A. It was then, very much so. I went away to have the baby in the dead of night and it was my mother and father, I love them dearly, and they are wonderful people, but they felt shame and of course that made me feel terribly guilty on top of everything else. And so I did as they asked me to do in terms of giving the baby up and keeping it all under wraps. Nowadays it's not quite that way and I'm glad that people are more open and honest about their feelings. I mean, let's face it, we're all human and make mistakes. I feel badly sometimes about what I put my mother and father through but then on the other hand sometimes I think that they let me down in terms of not giving me the psychological support that I needed. Otherwise they were wonderful but it was just a sense of shame. I don't feel that so much anymore.

Q. Let's go back to the time when you were pregnant with your daughter. Did you get counseling during this period of time?
A. In a way. Where I went was a home.

Q. You went to a maternity home?

A. Right. We did have one and I don't know why this doesn't come back to memory as clearly as other things. But we did have someone come in on occasion and talk with us but I don't remember it helping me all that much.

Q. Did you talk about your feelings?
A. Yes.

Q. Or did you talk about what you felt you needed to do, as far as making this decision?
A. I don't know what I was doing. Those were difficult times, some things were really clear and some things were really vague. I think that the things that stand out in my mind was the counseling not being that effective at the time. I remember I was older than a lot of girls that were there and so I sort of felt this sense of protectiveness for them and they sort of clung to me and we would meet in the hall or in someone's room and that was much more effective than any of the counseling for me. Just sitting there talking about our individual situations, sharing our feelings, that was a big help to me.

Q. Do you remember what your feelings were, did you vacillate back and forth as to what you were going to do or did you go one day at a time. . . .
A. I always knew I had the option of changing my mind and that's what got me through. I always knew that until I signed that paper, you know, I could go either way and I didn't make that decision until right before I signed the paper and made the final decision.

Q. Did you see the baby?
A. Yes.

Q. Did you hold the baby?
A. Yes.

Q. Do you recommend that to girls? To see the baby and to hold the baby?
A. For some, maybe. I guess it all depends on how deeply you feel. For me it was both a good thing and a bad thing. . . . All in all, I think overall I'm glad I did it. I don't think after going through all those months and making the decision I did, I'd ever really forgive myself if I had missed the opportunity because that was it. I can visualize her face and the feelings and everything

for a long time and then that fades. And now I'm glad I did. I guess overall I would recommend it, yes. Because you don't have that opportunity again and it's like saying hello and goodbye at the same time.

Q. Well a lot of women decide that they don't want to go through that kind of experience because it is so painful, but I think the general feeling, among professionals, is that you need to at least experience that situation so that you can really see the pregnancy as coming to an end and not having to go through life wondering what the baby looked like.

A. I think that would be more difficult. . . .

Q. I think from my point of view a lot of the unresolved loss is not ever having experienced the end of the pregnancy, refusing to look at the baby, refusing to acknowledge in a sense that there is a baby out there.

A. I remember that it was against the rules where I went to see the baby.

Q. Is that right?

A. Yes, and I broke the rules.

Q. Do you think that was a punitive thing?

A. There were a lot of things there that were that way. I mean, it was sort of, you know, backwoods, outdated, what word do I want? It's the way we were handled and treated. I could have thought of a lot of better ways to deal with someone who is in that situation and because of the rules I think most of the girls went along with it. I don't know of anyone else personally that broke the rule like I did but I had someone help me who cared about me then and I was allowed to do that then. I got in a little bit of trouble there doing it but it went through my mind what could they do to me, you know, this was my child and you have this little rule. And I mean, really, what can you do to me. So I did it anyway. I know one girl told me that it was like a dream for her. She was asleep during the delivery and she never saw her child, and for her it was like she couldn't just wipe it away. I don't know what happened to her later on but for her, she felt like she couldn't handle seeing her child, it would be too real. And this way it was like it was all a bad dream and it was over with and she could get on with her life. And I think maybe later she might have had some feelings about that, I don't know. I would have. I'm glad I did. . . .

Q. So you would recommend that she see the baby but not any prolonged period with the baby because that probably would not seem to help to let go.

A. Yes.

Q. What was the attitude that your parents had about giving the baby up, keeping the baby, etc., the decision you had to make.

A. There wasn't any question in their minds as far as they were concerned. It was the only thing I could do, as to give the baby up. I mean abortion was totally out of the question. I don't believe in it at all. At least it wasn't right for me.

Q. What are your thoughts about after all these years?

A. I do think about the child, I have great respect for adoptive parents and my hopes and dreams for the child are for the proverbial good life. she certainly deserves every bit of that.

Unmarried mothers are not of a single variety. The mothers presented here may not even be typical of all birth mothers. But there is a common thread (of loss) that comes through with the three dialogues presented here. To the extent that these cases are generalized, a certain poignant sensitivity about the child comes through, and an everpresent concern about the child for many years after the adoption proceedings have been finalized.

CHAPTER 11

RESEARCH IN ADOPTION

T ruth is a funny thing. Everyone seems to claim to have a "handle" on it, but when it really comes down to it, what is felt to be the truth is no more than a perception (of the truth) at best, a myth or an outright lie at worst. Statistics can be manipulated to support whatever one wishes to confirm or to prove.

That is the way it is with the state of the art in adoption practice. Much of the so-called "theory" in adoption practice comes to us from clinical impressions of practitioners, based on a clinic sample of people with a psychosocial or psychiatric disorder (who coincidentally happen to be adopted). The theory has not been tested in an empirical sense, but has, nevertheless, survived over the years as if it were truth.

One illustration of this phenomenon that clearly comes to mind is the "matching" principle in adoption. The idea underlying matching was to attempt to imitate nature as best as possible. Agencies have attempted, and still do to a considerable extent, to match the child with his perspective parents, not only physically, but in terms of educational values, standards, and expectations. This makes perfectly good sense on the face of it and the practice became an inviolable procedure of sound adoption practices. However, research findings on adoption outcome and matching reveals no relationship whatsoever. In other words, those placements characterized by the matching process turned out to be no different than those in which matching was not used (Ripple, 1968).

Another example relates to the sealed record issue. As stated earlier, it was based on a privacy theory. It was based on the view, rightly or wrongly, that the sealing of the records symbolized a new beginning for the adoptive family—that all parties in the adoption triangle, including the birth mother, would be best off in the long run. It was based on the "best interest of the child" philosophy. Now many parties are claiming that what was thought to be in the best interest of the child, in fact, was not. They claimed that they had empirical findings to confirm their view. They used the argument that many adoptees are searching for their birth parents in order to put to rest confused and ambiguous feelings about their personal identities. However, the reader should note that much of the so-called knowledge about the general characteristics of adoptees contain a serious methodological flaw. This is the error of attempting to generalize the findings of a clinic population to a non-clinic population. In this particular example, you cannot draw conclusions based on the findings of a group of emotionally disturbed people who happen to be adopted and generalize these findings to all adoptees. The most basic of all research principles is that you can only generalize the findings to a population like this one. The same error would be made if we hand-picked the most intelligent, well-adjusted, successful people in the world, found out which ones were adopted, administered a well-known standardized personality inventory, and then paraded the results as generalizable to all adoptees. The ludicrousness of such biased sampling should now be understood to the reader.

Ideally, the way to conduct research on adoptive subjects (using people from all three sides of the triangle) is to have a pool from which one can select on a random basis. For example, if a researcher had a pool of 100 birth mothers selected at random from a large heterogeneous group of birth mothers, s/he could generalize the findings to other birth mothers. This is because, in the random selection process, all important variables are considered to be randomly distributed, and people with certain characteristics would be counterbalanced in the long run by the selection of other members with the opposite set of characteristics. We know that this occurs when random procedures are used with a large enough sample. But it is not very practical or realistic to attempt to select such a sample since these people, birth mothers, in particular, have been guaranteed privacy and anonymity for the rest of their lives. This guarantee of anonymity may be true to a lesser extent with the other two groups but the principle of privacy still holds. What we see, then, are research findings on adoption from biased samples; i.e., people who volunteer to be research subjects. This procedure does not make the findings worthless but provide limitations in interpretation of the data.

Consequently, it is not surprising that there have only been few systematic efforts to examine the impact of adoption itself or current adoption practices upon the development of the child. It is a difficult process for the researcher to isolate the factor of adoptive status from all the other factors affecting a child's adjustment. A standard research text (Kerlinger, 1964) presents the problem quite succinctly:

> It is not always possible for a researcher to formulate his problems simply, clearly, and completely. He may often have a rather general, diffuse, even confused notion of the problem. This is in the nature of the complexity of scientific research (p. 18.).

Thus, the multiplicity of the interrelated variables and limitations in the sample itself present formidable problems in ferreting out the myriad factors associated with success or failure in adoption. They pose problems in interpretation of the presently available data. They also present formidable obstacles in obtaining answers to questions of interest to those in the adoption field. In brief, the lot of the researcher is to rule out the alternative explanations for the phenomenon under investigation. To put it another way, he must convince himself (and others) that what he thinks is responsible for the occurrence of the phenomenon is truly responsible and not something else.

There has been considerable speculation that the adoptive child is more prone to develop psychiatric problems. The evidence supporting this alleged vulnerability is that adoptees are disproportionately represented in caseloads of mental health practitioners. But this argument is disputed by those who point out certain methodological flaws. Madison, for example, rejected the claim on this basis:

> In making comparisons with non-adopted children, the wrong population base is used: no allowance is made for race or urban residence, although it is well-known that clinics are largely situated in cities in certain parts of the country; no heed is paid to the economic status, although the adoptive parents described obviously had money enough (which is not always the case) to obtain psychiatric help. That adoptive parents might have less hesitance about seeking psychiatric help than natural parents is not taken into account. (p. 257).

There may be some value in elaborating some of the methodological problems or flaws cited by Madison which frequently are overlooked in the interpretation of findings, not the least of which is the fact that certain coincidental sociocultural differences between adopted and non-adopted families were overlooked.

1. The problem of self-selection is a limiting factor in properly evaluating research results. The problem of self-selection is that when people are drawn into a sample because they possess a particular characteristic of which the investigator is unaware, there is a lack of control of other factors which may be intruding into the particular phenomenon under the investigation.

2. Adoptive families tend to be well-educated, upper-middle class and success oriented. Having sought out an agency (or other professionals) to obtain a child, they are more likely to seek the services of professionals whenever the situation calls for it.

3. In various studies, there is variation in the degree of methodological precision, the phenomenon measured, the criteria for evaluating adoptive outcome, and the statistics employed. Among the list of outcome measures are parental satisfaction, parental ratings of the child's interpersonal adjustment, ratings of the adoptive relative to his relationship with his (adoptive) parents, academic performance of the child, and the quality of the parent-child relationship. Variation in the methodology includes the methods used in obtaining data, the sources of such data, the types of samples used, and statistical measures used in evaluating outcome.

Before examining some of the research finding as they pertain to adoption, it may be well to digress just for a moment to explain some terminology or jargon used in research reports. The terms "significance" generally refers to statistical significance, and is related to the notion of "probability."

The concept of probability is useful in deciding whether one's sample findings are meaningful enough to lead one to the conclusion that there really is a relationship between the two variables under examination. In other words, we are concerned with the level of probability that an observed finding would occur if, in truth, there really was no relationship between the two variables under study (technically called the null hypothesis). Its value, which ranges from .00 to .99, tells us how many chances out of a hundred that a particular finding would have occurred by chance. Thus the designation "$p = .05$" means that such a finding would occur by chance 5 times in 100 if there really is no relationship. In other words, the stronger the relationship, the smaller the probability (p). To summarize, the term "probability" has a specific meaning in evaluating out-come findings. If one adopts a decision level of .05 (which has been the conventional level of significance), then one will consider any relationship with a higher p (.10 or .15, for example) as accounted for by chance, and therefore not real. Any differences with probability of .05 or less (.03, .01, for example) would be considered too large to be accounted for by chance and are, therefore, considered to be "real."

As previously stated, it has been reported that a disproportionate number of adoptees are seen in psychiatric clinics, but there remains some controversy over whether there are psychological conflicts which are specific to the adoption situation. Adopted children do somehow need to face and resolve some rather complex identity issues and this has been reported in the literature (Schechter, 1964; Sorosky, Baran, Pannor, 1975). Kadushin, a nationally recognized child welfare researcher, noted that 98% of adopted children have never been referred for psychiatric treatment (1966). Further, those cases selected on a random basis, or through a matching procedure (to ensure comparability of groups), suggest few differences, if any, between adopted and nonadopted populations. It would appear that on the face of it, adoptees are seen with greater frequency than one would expect. On the other hand, a number of studies which use larger samples and accepted scientific procedure bear results that demonstrate that, with few exceptions, adopted children develop as physically and emotionally stable as their non-adoptive peers. One might entertain the idea that differences in the methodology result in differences in outcome.

Nevertheless, certain findings have contributed significantly to our understanding of adoption and it might be helpful to examine more closely the differences between families who do require professional help and those who do not. For those who do receive services related to adoption, there are a variety of reasons.

1. Problems of unresolved infertility (for example, "I still can't help feeling resentful whenever I see a pregnant woman.")

2. Problems revolving around entitlement (for example, "I keep asking myself if I have a right to him.")

3. Problems of the parents' disappointment over growth and development issues; and

4. Problems inherent in learning of diagnosis of neurological or intellectual impairment.

These difficulties may play themselves out in the parent-child relationship with the result that the parents are viewed as over-protective and overdefensive in regard to handling the child.

There may be another group whose difficulties are not related to adoption but, because the child is adopted, it is easy for the nonresearch oriented clinician to blame the difficulty on the fact of the adoptive status. In this category fall the myriad situations in which communication among family members is contradictory, dishonest, and/or destructive. Parents who use their children as pawns for fighting with each other invariably produce a situation in which the children become troubled and therefore come to the attention of those in the mental health field. This group might also include those family situations in which parents feel guilty (for whatever reason or constellation of reasons) in their day-to-day contacts with the child, the child perceives the guilt and works it to his/her advantage. It would seem, then, that the greater incidence of emotional disturbance is not related to the adoption per se, but to consequent difficulties in the parent-child relationship.

Having cautioned the reader against drawing hasty conclusions based on the interpretations of existing findings, we now may proceed to examine some studies which may be of interest to adoptive parents. In a fairly recent study at a large midwestern high school, Sandra Smith compared a group of adoptees with a group of non-adoptees, matching them on sex, age, and religious affiliation. She found that both groups were favorable toward opening the records, but that the non-adoptees were more interested in opening the sealed records than were the adoptees ($p = .15$). Further, she found the adoptees expressing a greater sense of obligation to their parents than their non-adoptive counterparts (p = .07).

There are two studies universally cited in any treatise on the subject of the research. These are reported by Triseliotis, a social worker in Scotland, who interviewed 70 Scottish adoptees who had contacted the appropriate searching agency in Edinburgh, seeking information about their background and origins. Sorosky, et.al. reported on interviews with about 50 adult adoptees who had completed reunions with their biological parents.

A detailed review of the Scottish study revealed that the adoptive parents, as a whole, violated the prescriptive standard of adoptions practice regarding telling. Nearly two-thirds of the children first learned about the adoption when they were eleven years of age or older, and when they did find out, the source was likely to be someone other than the adoptive parents. Age of learning about adoption was associated with satisfaction in their relationship with their parents, with younger-age children expressing the greatest satisfaction and the older-age children the least satisfaction. For those over ten years of age, revelation of the adoption was perceived as a shock, requiring a new orientation of the self, concomitant with intense anger at their adoptive parents. The reader should realize, however, that this was a biased sample and not one from which to draw generalizations to all adoptees. In spite of this shortcoming, the research points out the importance of many of the points made earlier in our book about how adoptees should be told, the age of telling and by whom they should be told.

In many respects, the Triseliotis findings were mirrored by those of Sorosky, Baran and Pannor. They studied meetings between adoptees and birth parents as a result of contacts solicited through newspaper accounts of their interest. They, too, experienced revelation concerning adoption relatively later in life and learned about the adoption by someone other than their parents in one-third of the cases. Most of them, as in the case of the Triseliotis study, saw the meeting with their birth parents as advantageous. Most reported a sense of closure and completeness in regard to identity issues. Most saw the meeting as beneficial and none saw it as an attempt to replace their adoptive parents. Rather, they reported, as a result of the meeting, a deeper sense of love for their adoptive parents, who they viewed as their "psychological parents."

In both of these studies, females were found more likely to engage in search than males. It is interesting to speculate on what might be the cause of this phenomenon. There may be some valid explanations for this distribution, however. It may be that women, as future childbearers, are more sensitive to the issue of discontinuity of the biological line. Another explanation may be the fact that, in our society, women may be more encouraged to express their true feelings about identity concerns. It is not that men do not share such concerns, but their overt expression may be less acceptable than for women.

In a recent study (Kowal and Schilling, 1985), 110 adult adoptees contacted their placement agency or a search group during a calendar year period of 1982–83. Although a non-representative (of all adoptees) group, their findings showed some similarities and some differences from the previous two studies cited. In this study, one-fourth reported that they were given very little information about their own genetic background. An additional 6 percent added marginal comments indicative of their dissatisfaction with information given or that it had subsequently proved to be untrue.

This parallels the Triseliotis and Sorosky, et.al., studies regarding background information. On the other hand, 60 percent of the subjects reported having been told of the adoption at an early age, heeding the prescriptive standard for early telling. An additional 29 percent reported not being told until their elementary school years. This would seem to indicate some salient differences between this study and the previous two studies identified.

One of the most interesting questions addressed in this study was the feelings of adoptees about being adopted. Books written for adoptive parents have almost universally advised the appropriateness of the word "chosen" or "special" in the telling (for example, see Raymond, 1955). However, Kirk (1964) takes the position that adoption carries with it some degree of "role handicap." The emphasis on chosenness, he claims, is an attempt to cover up the feelings of being disadvantaged. In the study being reported, 35 percent reported feeling chosen or special; 22 percent reported feeling no different from anyone else; 21 percent reported feeling different, but neither better nor worse than others; 25 percent reported being worried about it; and 17 percent reported feelings of embarrassment. Thus, there was a range of attitudes, and it is perhaps most interesting that 57 percent of the adoptees felt reasonably positive about adoption. (Remember that this was a sample of adoptees who contacted the agencies responsible for their placement.)

Much has been written about identity conflicts of adolescent adoptees and many of the theoretical concerns are identified in a previous chapter (6). Sorosky and his colleagues believed that their findings support their belief that adoptees are more vulnerable than the general population to identity conflicts in late adolescence and early adulthood. (Again, we remind the reader of the cautions against generalizing from a clinic population. In fact, in a recent study of adoptees matched for comparison with a group of non-adoptees revealed no discernible differences in identity scores [Stein and Hoopes, 1985]).

This finding parallels an interesting study of identity crises of both adoptees and non-adoptees, as reported by Norvell and Guy (1977). In comparing self-concept scores between the two groups, they found no significant differences, and concluded:

> Adoptive status itself cannot produce a negative identity. If negative elements become incorporated in the adolescent's identity, they more likely than not stem from problems within the home (p. 445).

Other research efforts yield similar results. In a recent comparison between searchers and non-searchers (looking for critical differences between the two groups), the non-searchers had a more positive self-image than the searchers (Aumend and Barrett, 1984).

Loper (1976) was interested in comparing searchers and non-searchers, not on the basis of identity issues, but on key personality factors and social variables. Breaking her sample down to three separate groups (from those having no interest in their biological parents to those whose interest was active), she concluded the following:

1. Non-searchers had more positive self-concepts than searchers ($p = .01$);)

2. Non-searchers had more positive attitudes toward their adoptive parents. They viewed their adoptive parents as more emotionally involved in a positive way than did searchers;

3. Although the non-searchers learned of their adoption at an earlier age than their counterpart searchers, the difference was not statistically significant;

4. Concerning a rating of "overall happiness," a disproportionate number of non-searchers reported a "very happy" or "mostly happy" life (90 percent) compared with
searchers (41 percent); and

5. Non-searchers began living with their adoptive family at
an earlier age than did searchers. Nearly 90 percent of the
non-searchers were placed prior to 6 months of age compared to 80 percent of the searchers.

Overall, the study seems to cast doubt on the alleged vulnerability of all adoptees. Based on the study findings, adoptees
tend to have positive self-concepts, are reasonably satisfied with
their relationships with their parents, and revealed critical differences between searchers and non-searchers.

While there is much we do not know relative to adoption
success, there is much we do know. We know that the vast majority of adoptive placements are successful, that boys are more
likely than girls to develop some form of conduct disorders
(whether this has anything to do with the adoption is not known),
but girls are more likely to search. We know that children with
a history of previous deprivations and multiple placements,
especially within their first two years of life, are at a higher risk
of adoption failure. We know that adoptions in which the adoptive parents have excessive expectations of the child are at a high
risk.

A number of variables, previously thought to have a bearing on outcome and, therefore, became major issues in agency
adoption practice, proved to have no basis in fact. These include:
background factors in the child; adoptive parents' age; length of
marriage; income and educational level; socio-economic status;
and religion. As stated previously, attempts to match infants'
potential with parents' characteristics and expectations, proved
unsuccessful. The principal factors seem to be parental attitudes
toward the child—their unconditional acceptance of him and the
degree to which they have worked through feelings of entitlement.

A number of variables, it seems rather evident, offers no clear
picture of how to best tell a child of his origins. We believe,
however, based for the most part on our findings, that the age-
old practice of telling the child while he is young is assuredly advisable, provided it is not overdone and is not done inappropriate-
ly. The evidence is strong that that parent-child relationship which
is one of loving and caring is the best predictor of the most satisfac-
tory outcome.

CHAPTER 12

ATTITUDES TOWARD THE SEALED RECORD: AN EMPIRICAL STUDY*

There is a particular scenario that is played out on television and made-for-TV movies. It portrays an adolescent female adoptee in feverish pursuit of her birth mother. The scenario usually contains the following sequence of events:

1. In initiating her search, she encounters rigid and arbitrary institutional barriers in regard to the birth mothers identity. Anguish and frustration are experienced repeatedly, anguish in regard to the need to locate, and frustration over the massive resistance she encounters.

2. She becomes resigned to her fate and is just about to abandon her search efforts when, "out of the blue," a breakthrough occurs as a result of a breakdown of confidentiality.

3. Contact is made, sometimes under camouflage or subterfuge, and the girl reveals her adoptive status to the birth mother, who, in turn, is taken aback, denying she is the person the girl thinks she is. Irritation and anger may characterize the birth mother's response.

4. Disappointed and crestfallen, refusing to believe a mistake was made but privately acknowledging such a possibility, the adoptee returns home to salve her wounds.

5. Unexpectedly, the birth mother shows up at the home of the searcher, with apologies for refusing to acknowledge

*This study was carried out by Dr. Smith

her birth mother status. She seems open, explaining her earlier response on the basis of fear. She attempts to answer the inevitable "why she relinquished the child" and explains the birth father's non-involvement on the basis of his untimely death (automobile or motorcycle accident, usually).

Just how closely this scenario resembles the reality of the situation is in doubt. In reality, the searcher may or may not be successful in the search efforts and many do find some satisfaction with the effort. In actuality, we know more about the searcher, if there is a prototype, than the non-searcher. At any rate, there is a need to find out more information about the attitudes of all those involved in the adoption triangle.

Some background information is in order at this point. The sealed record in adoptions is the subject of considerable controversy in child welfare circles and legislative bodies. The controversy basically centers around a conflict of rights between adoptees, birth parents and adoptive parents. In recent years, a public perception has emerged involving the desire of many adoptees to locate their birth parents. This perception is due largely to shifting ideological perspectives concerning adoption, and is supported by newspaper accounts and television programs in regard to a successful search. This perception includes a view that continued denial of access to original birth records causes unneeded psychological suffering and distress.

Opponents of the sealed record point of view usually begin their arguments with the observation that the sealed record position is in a state of flux. They go on to challenge the basic assumptions underlying the confidentiality and anonymity guarantees from both legal and psychological perspectives. From a legalistic vantage point, the contention is that the anonymity guarantees deny adoptees "equal protection under the law" because such (sealed record) procedures cause adoptees to be dealt with in discriminatory practices not experienced by non-adoptees. The argument concludes with the assertion that the agreement made between the placing parties and the adopters was made without the adoptee's consent.

Others object because of the psychological implications. They claim that denial of access to birth records inadvertently blocks the (adopted) adolescent from achieving a most crucial psychological task, the achievement of his identity (Erikson, 1950). All adolescents, of course, face the problem of defining for themselves who they really are. For the adolescent who is adopted, the process of self-identification is made more difficult and complex because of the need to incorporate the image of two different sets of parent figures. The term "genealogical bewilderment" has been used in the literature to describe certain perceived gaps in their psychological self-image (Sants, 1964).

Those who advocate continuance of the procedure (of sealed records) cite the relative disinterest of most adoptees of any procedural change. The unsealing of the records represents a violation of confidentiality and the anonymity extended to both the adoptive parents and the birth parents. For the birth parents, having made what was believed to be a final decision, the anticipation was that the matter was a "closed chapter." For the adoptive parents, who were also promised privacy, the fear of the loss of confidentiality is accompanied by a fear of the loss of the child.

The significance of the problem is both a state problem (as adoption practices are covered by state law) and a national problem. Because of its significance to the public, the legislature and to social agencies, it is necessary to cull opinions and attitudes of those most closely identified with the sealed record controversy.

There is a paucity of information available on this subject matter. While various theoretical positions have been stated, none provide data to support said positions. Therefore, this study was done to provide a more systematic evaluation of the three different groups of the adoption triangle, (i.e., adoptive parents, birth parents and adoptees) and their attitudes toward the sealed record.

The total sample size was 107. Although a larger group, particularly in the birth parent and adoptee categories would have been desirable, it simply was not possible. A deliberate decision was made not to include subjects who had identified themselves as members of a particular organization (as searchers or nonsearchers). This would have skewed the sample to a rather remarkable degree and made the findings ungeneralizable. On the other hand, if a subject agreed to take part in the study and subsequently revealed his/her membership in a search organization, this was found to be acceptable. The main point of a diversified sample is to keep the group as heterogeneous as possible in order to enhance its generalizability.

CHARACTERISTICS OF RESPONDENTS

Table 1

	Adoptive Parents	Birth Parents	Adoptees
1. Age			
a. mean	40	36	29.5
b. median	43	37	29
c. range	28–68	20–50	13–51
2. Gender			
a. male	17	0	10
b. female	40	20	20
3. Race	White	White	White
4. Average Educational Level	Between college and college grad	Between high school and college	Between college and college grad
5. Average Level of Occupation	Between managerial and white collar	Between white collar and blue collar	Between managerial and white collar
6. Level of Family Income	$23,001 and over	$17,000–$30,000	$23,000 and over

As Table 1 indicates, the sample sizes are as follows: adoptive parents, 57; birth parents, 20; and adoptees, 30. The median age (which is the mid-point in each distribution) is reported as 43, 37 and 29 respectively. There are no birth fathers in the sample and all respondents are white. (This was not by design but by happenstance.)

The table also shows a continuum in regard to educational level, occupational level and family income. As one might expect, there is a distinct similarity between the adoptive parents and the adoptees, which is slightly higher than the birth parents group.

Because there were three separate groups included in this study, it was essential to design a questionnaire that would adequately apply to each group. However, because each of these three groups had its own unique position within the adoption triangle, three separate questionnaires were developed in order to tailor the questions to each group satisfactorily. All three questionnaires used a Likert-type scale ranging from 1 to 5. Answers to all questions ranged from strong disagreement to strong agreement with each respondent being offered a choice on this continuum.

Since there was not just one particular question on the questionnaires that best represented the respondents' attitudes toward the sealed records, a summary score was developed. This was based on nine of the questions that were asked of all the respondents on their separate questionnaires. This summary score, then, best represented the global attitude of the respondents toward the sealed record. The higher the summary score for each respondent, the more the respondent was in favor of opening sealed records. On the other hand, the lower the summary score, the more the respondent was in favor of keeping records sealed. The highest possible summary score was 45 (i.e., answering "5" or "Strongly Agree" on each of the nine questions dealing with the respondents' attitude toward sealed records). The lowest possible score was "9," which meant the respondent answered all nine questions with a "1" or "Strongly Disagree." In contrast, then, a low score represented an attitude that sealed records should remain sealed, while a high score meant a "pro-open" attitude toward sealed records.

Below is a list of the nine questions asked of all the respondents:

1. Any person who is part of the adoption process should have the right of access to sealed records containing confidential information about the adoption.

2. I would be in favor of discontinuing the agency practice (where it exists) of destroying confidential information about an adoptee after a certain number of years following the adoption.

3. I like the idea of a registry for those adoptees and birth parents who would like to contact each other.

4. Sealed record procedures violate the constitutional right of an adoptee to have access to information.

*5. If adoptees were given sufficient non-identifying information about the birth parents and adoption, this would probably satisfy most of the potential searchers.

*6. I think that adoption records should be permanently sealed, with no exceptions.

*7. Adoptees who search for birth parents are generally more unhappy about being adopted than those who do not search.

*8. Responsibility for releasing adoption records should rest only with the court on a case-by-case basis.

*9. Media accounts of "the search" usually give a distorted account of what might occur should an adoptee and birth parent meet.

As seen above, some of the questions were stated with a "pro-open" attitude toward sealed records and some were worded with a "pro-closed" attitude (those marked within [*] asterisk). The reason for doing this is to prevent the respondents from answering questions in one particular pattern or mind set. By arranging the wording of the questions to break such patterns, the questionnaire helps to safeguard against response set bias. However, when developing the summary score, in order for all the scores to be going in the same direction, those answers given to the "pro-closed" questions were reversed when scoring. For example, if the respondent scored a question with a 1, it was rescored as 5; 2 was rescored as 4; 4 rescored as 2; 5 rescored as 1; and 3 was left unchanged (Fischer, 1978). Then, all the scores for the nine questions were added up for each of the respondents, which resulted in a summary score that best represented the respondent's attitude toward sealed records.

The percentages of respondents in each of the three groups that had a low summary score (i.e., 9–27) and a high summary score (i.e., 28–45) are given in the table below:

SUMMARY SCORES

Table 2

Respondent	9–27 low	28–45 high
Adoptive parents	40%	60%
Birth parents	5%	95%
Adoptees	20%	80%

As the chart indicates, 40 percent of the adoptive parents who responded gave a score of 27 or below, representing a "pro-closed" attitude toward sealed records, while 60 percent of the adoptive parents had a score of 28 or above, indicating a "pro-open" attitude toward sealed records. This sharply contrasts with the responses of the birth parents, who had only 5 percent of the respondents with scores of 27 or below, and 95 percent of them with scores of 28 and above. The adoptees position reflected a middle position between the other two groups with 20 percent of the respondents with low summary scores of 27 or less and 80 percent with high scores of 28 or more.

The average summary score for each of the three groups is also given in the chart below:

Table 3

Respondents	Average Summary Score
Adoptive parents	27.2
Birth parents	35.5
Adoptees	31.0

Table 3 reflects the attitudinal positions of all three groups. This is another way of casting the data presented in Table 2. In essence, the adoptive parents' group is most in favor of continuing to keep records closed while the birth parents group favors opening them up. And as stated earlier, the adoptees are almost exactly in the middle. What is significant about this finding is that neither the adoptive parent group nor the birth parent group are at the extremes (as one might expect). Remember that an ideal pro-closed score would be 9; an ideal pro-open score would be 45. That there is such latitude in the scores reflects some recognition on all parts of the complexities involved.

Inasmuch as there is a significant difference between the three groups, we then wondered whether each group differed from each other to a significant degree. The following table reflects these differences, all found to be significant:

Table 4 SUMMARY SCORE/ADOPTIVE PARENTS
AND BIRTH PARENTS

Group	Mean	N	Level of Significance
1	27.211	57	
2	35.500	20	p = .001

SUMMARY SCORE/ADOPTIVE PARENTS AND
ADOPTEES

Group	Mean	N	Level of Significance
1	27.211	57	
2	32.033	30	p = .001

SUMMARY SCORE/BIRTH PARENTS AND ADOPTEES

Group	Mean	N	Level of Significance
1	35.500	20	
2	31.033	30	p = .02

To further explain the three groups' attitudes toward sealed records, the following chart will list the nine questions used to compile the summary score and the average response given by each of the three groups for each of the separate questions.

1 Strongly Disagree
2 Disagree
3 Undecided
4 Agree
5 Strongly Agree

Table 5 AVERAGE SCORE FOR THE NINE SUMMARY QUESTIONS

Questions	Adoptive Parents	Birth Parents	Adoptees	Are Differences Significant?
1. Any person who is part of the adoption process should have the right to access sealed records	2.3	3.5	3.0	yes
2. I am in favor of discontinuing the agency practice of destroying confidential information	3.6	4.4	3.9	no

3. I like the idea of a registry for those adopt-ees and birth parents who would like to con-tact each other	4.0	4.5	4.0	no
4. Sealed record procedures violate the constitutional right of an adoptee	2.7	4.0	3.8	yes
5. If adoptees were given sufficient non-identify-ing information about the birth parents and the adoption, this would probably satisfy most of the potential searchers (reverse score)	2.5	3.7	2.7	yes
6. I think that adoption records should be per-manently sealed, with no exceptions (reverse score)	3.9	4.7	4.4	yes
7. Adoptees who search for birth parents are general-ly more happy ... (reverse score)	3.1	4.4	3.6	yes
8. Responsibility for releas-ing adoption records should rest only with the court on a case-by-case basis (reverse score)	3.0	3.6	3.1	no
9. Media accounts of "the search" usually give a distorted account of what might occur should an adoptee and birth parent meet (reverse score)	2.2	2.8	2.6	yes

Note: Those questions marked with "reverse score" indicates the revers-ing of scores.

The reader may think it unusual that the birth parent group reflected the most extreme position on all nine of the sealed record questions. The findings should put to rest any assumption that the decision to place the child for adoption represented a "closed chapter" in their lives. For most, if not all, there remains some feelings of anger attendant to the decision to give the child up for adoption.

The reader should note the same pattern with respect to the three groups. Differences are significant for all three groups on most of these questions. Differences were not significant in three areas: (1) the agency practice of destroying confidential information; (2) favoring a voluntary registry; and (3) releasing adoption records to be left to the court on a case-by-case basis.

Examination of adoptive parents' attitudes suggest the perpetration of a myth regarding their feelings associated with the telling. Many authors have previously commented on the problematic nature of telling, suggesting that this is a time of mounting anxiety for adoptive parents for a variety of reasons (see chapter 6). Our data suggest, however, a majority (better than 60 percent) found the telling to be a quite satisfying experience. While an additional third (35 percent) were not sure about their feelings, or their children were too young to be told, it is significant that only two respondents (3 percent of the sample) found the telling dissatisfying.

Adopters were asked what feelings they might have in regard to a possible search initiated by their children. This statement yielded a mixed picture, with responses at all points along the continuum. However, most of the respondents, or 53 percent, disagreed that such a search stirred up anxious feelings in them. Many of the adopters noted that it was not the fact of the search they objected to, but the fear that their child might be hurt in the process. (The idea of voluntary registry was much more acceptable to them, as 74 percent expressed approval of such a mechanism.)

The remainder of the study will focus on the attitudes of the adoptees toward the sealed record. This area of inquiry seems particularly pertinent inasmuch as the adopted adolescent has been portrayed as unhappy, confused, and angry over having been denied access to birth records. Identity conflicts have been reported in the literature as particularly applicable to the adolescent and young adult adoptee. While it has not been our intent to debunk or reject such theoretical arguments, we found it desirable to obtain findings that might shed some light on the validity of such assertions. Accordingly, we present the following table:

Table 6   ADOPTEES ATTITUDES TOWARD ADOPTION

	Agree	Undecided	Disagree
1. I have experienced pain in my life because I am adopted.	14 (47%)	0	16 (53%)
2. My parents were sensitive to my needs about matters pertaining to my adoption.	20 (67%)	5 (16%)	5 (16%)
3. I think adoptees have a greater sense of gratitude to their parents than non-adoptees.	10 (32%)	11 (37%)	9 (30%)
4. The agency (or lawyer) that placed me provided my family with adequate background information.	12 (40%)	6 (20%)	12 (40%)
5. Adoptees have a more difficult time developing their identity than non-adoptees.	10 (33%)	4 (13%)	16 (53%)
6. Up to the present time, I would say that my life has been satisfying.	24 (80%)	2 (7%)	4 (13%)
7. The fact of my adoption has never made me feel different from other people.	14 (47%)	1 (3%)	15 (50%)
8. My parents were comfortable (not anxious) in discussing adoption with me.	21 (70%)	2 (7%)	7 (23%)

9. In general, my relationship with my adoptive parents has been a positive one.	26 (87%)	3 (10%)	1 (3%)
10. For the most part, I find myself wishing that I were a non-adoptee.	5 (17%)	1 (3%)	23 (80%)

The above table displays the responses given by the adoptees on their attitudes toward adoption. The majority of the adoptees seem to have had positive experiences in their adoption. For most of the questions there was a higher percentage of respondents that answered positively in regards to their adoption.

These data do not support the view that adoptees are at any greater risk than the general population. For the most part, the adoptee's adjustment parallels the adjustment of other reports of adoptive outcome (Ripple, 1968). The data do suggest, however, some feelings about being adopted ("feeling different from other people"), particularly those who received only a paucity of information given to their adoptive parents by the placing agency. When you consider that only 40 percent of the adoptees felt that the background information given was adequate, that says something about adoptive placement practice and procedure that should be given weightier consideration.

The findings are also consistent with previous reports of a relationship between sealed record attitudes and gender. For some reason or host of reasons, females are more interested in searching and we found this to be the case as well (p = .02). Other gender differences in the study relate to agreement with the statement that "adoptees have a greater sense of gratitude toward their parents than non-adoptees" with 10 percent of the males agreeing compared to 45 percent of the females. Males were much less likely to admit to wishing he were a non-adoptee (11 percent to 21 percent).

SUMMARY

This study was designed to provide answers to attitudes toward the sealed record. The major conclusion was that attitudes of the three groups differed along expected lines. While birth parents expressed the strongest pro-open views and adoptive parents expressed the strongest pro-closed views, these attitudes were not extreme and recognized the complexity involved for all concerned. Certainly one area of agreement was the desire for a voluntary registry as a way of accommodating those whose needs for finding out more information are more pressing.

It is true that many of the birth mothers would like to make contact with the children they gave up years ago but at the same time recognize that this decision must rest with the adoptees. One must remember that for the most part, these placements occurred at a time in our history in which keeping a child (born out of wedlock) was not a viable option.

For the adoptee, it does not appear that he/she has done a great deal of thinking in regard to the adoption, but that adoption has had an impact on their lives. The greatest need, from their point of view, is to have adequate background information so that the genetic and experiential components of their life histories can be more readily integrated. At the same time, the vast majority are satisfied with the way their lives have developed and they have enjoyed a positive relationship with their parents.

The implication of these findings present formidable challenges to researchers in the future. While the methodology could have been more rigorous, the very fact of promised anonymity to this group of subjects presents inherent difficulties in obtaining a truly representative sample. Further, there is the problem of self-selection, which is always to be considered as a factor capable of jeopardizing the validity of the findings.

Nevertheless, efforts were made to provide more reliable responses through follow-up telephone calls. While most adoptees are not actively considering a search, they do think about their genetic heritage. The factor most clearly identified as related to the search seems to be their access (or lack thereof) to background information. Likewise, while many birth mothers are desirous of a reunion, there is a prevailing view that they would honor the agreement made at the time of placement, however great the emotional price they would have to pay.

CHAPTER 13

A CLOSING NOTE

M uch has been said about the difficulties involved in the adoptive parenting role. The literature on the subject abounds with references to competing with phantom figures, dealing belatedly with the various forms of narcissistic wounds, and covering up basic feelings of emptiness with a host of self-reassuring messages about one's own worthiness in being selected to parent a given child. Unfortunately, many of these tasks are, in reality, as they have been presented—difficult at best, impossible at worst. Yet most adoptive parents would tell you that these tasks are overplayed and that parenting a child one adopts is essentially no different than any other form of parenting and that the joys and hazards of parenting transcend the adoption issue. In most adoptive families, adoption surfaces on rare occasions, usually in response to a remark made by a neighbor about who the child looks like or in response to a made-for-TV movie utilizing the adoption theme (such as a teenage girl searching out her birth parents). While these situations do occur, and in some cases with a good deal of regularity, it has been our experience that such phenomena are rare in most families which have dealt effectively with their feelings related to adoption.

Historically, we have noticed an increasing willingness on the part of parents to discuss adoption with their children with overtones of pleasure and positive parenting; however, this was not always, or even primarily, the case as adoption was practiced in the early 60's. At that time we had many babies to place and standards were greatly relaxed to accommodate the number of infants that were available for adoption. In those days, the stigma associated with illegitimacy and the humiliation surrouding the circumstances of the conception heightened people's sensitivities to the adoption issue. It was not an unusual occurrence at that time to provide the adoptive parents with background information on the child, at which time many of these parents stated that they were not interested in such information. One has to wonder how they handled the child's need for information of his genetic past during the child's developmental milestones. Another development is the tendency to dilute the anonymity associated with the adoption and sealed record process. Certainly, the media has exploited many adoptees' need to find birth parents as well as birth parents' need to find children they gave up years ago. States are becoming more responsive to such requests, aided by the various search groups and organizations, and legislatures are progressively setting up voluntary registers where various parties in the adoption triangle find each other if there is mutual consent. Then the whole "open adoption" concept does away completely with the anonymity previously afforded and this practice can have far reaching effects for adoptive parents and children alike. This practice is currently being evaluated.

We believe that the single most unique task in adoptive parenthood is the development of the feeling that the child really belongs to them. This phenomenon has been referred to as "entitlement." The sense of entitlement of the parents to the child, of the child to the parent, and siblings to each other is a task unique to adoption. This sense of entitlement, or belongingness, if you will, refers not only to the perceptions that the child really belongs to them but that in addition, he or she belongs to them unconditionally and even exclusively. Now this is a relatively easy procedure when one has a biological child and the sense of entitlement for a biological parent probably occurs at an unconscious level. But for adoptive parents, there is that extra psychological step to take because the adoptive parents know that the child was brought into the world, in reality, by another set of people.

The building blocks of successful adoption are communication, acceptance and a strong, secure sense of identity. In a close, nurturing family, these factors emerge together. Communication is perhaps the most important, because open communication is necessary for the development of both acceptance and a sense of identity.

Parents who are able to discuss adoption in a direct, honest manner teach their children that adoption is acceptable. It is not necessary and, in fact, it is undesirable that all family communication revolve around adoption. The subject should be neither dwelled upon nor totally avoided. There is a comfortable middle ground where adoption is acknowledged as a fact and discussed when it is appropriate. When the parent continually brings up the adoption in unrelated conversation, the parent is likely suffering from unresolved anxieties and will communicate these feelings to the child. The parent who purposely avoids discussing adoption often harbors unresolved conflicts, as well, and may unknowingly send his child the message that adoption is unacceptable. Too much or too little communication regarding the adoption may cause the child to question his own desirability and jeopardize his rightful place within the family unit.

The adopted child and his parents will have feelings about adoption. The child will likely voice fears and concerns and ask questions about his adoption from an early age. Parents who acknowledge and accept their child's feelings put their child on the road to developing a healthy self-identity. And parents who answer their child's questions in a direct, sincere and loving manner teach the child acceptance of himself and his place in the family situation.

The ease with which the child accepts his adoptedness is directly related to the degree of success the adoptive parents have had in accepting their own status of adoptive parents. Thus, it is imperative for them to accept their new parenting roles and develop a sense of entitlement to the child if the child is to grow up feeling good about himself.

The parents' feelings about infertility can affect acceptance of the child. Hostility can replace love toward the child if the child is continually viewed as a symbol of biological inadequacy. Open communication between the couple and professional counseling may help resolve feelings about inadequacy. Such counseling toward resolution of problems associated with infertility should take place prior to the adoption of the child whenever possible. Those who come to the realization that sexual capacity must not be equated with producing a child can find great emotional satisfaction in their relationship and in the contribution they can make to a child's growth and development through adoptive parenthood.

A child who experiences honest, open communication and feels that his parents accept him becomes an integral part of the family unit. The child feels that he belongs and identifies himself with the family. The "telling" is important to the child's sense of identity. The adoptive parent who assures his child that "you are mine despite the fact that someone else gave birth to you" tells the child that his "real" family is his adoptive family. The child who is taught that adoption is good feels that he, too, is good. He comes to like himself and feels that he is a worthwhile and valuable part of the family. The child comes to see that those who care for and love him, and not those who gave birth to him, are, indeed, his parents.

While adoptees do often encounter difficulties developing a sense of self-identity and resolving the issue of rejection by their birth parents, so do other children, and these factors alone do not put adoptees at greater developmental risk than children living with their biological parents. Vastly more important to the growing child is not the fact of adoption, but the quality of family life in which he finds himself.

Problems are facts of life in even the most loving, accepting families. Families do not always function in harmonious accord. Friction between family members, particularly between children and their parents, must be anticipated and accepted as natural occurrences. It should not be avoided as if it could not or should not exist. For adoptive parents, it may be tempting to attribute parent-child conflict or a child's delayed or inappropriate social behavior to the adoption itself. It is extremely important, and also reassuring, to realize that the most common source of problems are developmental changes which follow a child from infancy to adulthood, not the fact that the child was or was not adopted.

Adoption practice today is truly in a state of flux. Experts disagree on such issues as open adoption and transracial adoption. The decade of the 70's brought monumental and revolutionary changes to the practice of adoption. One of these pertains to the rights of birth parents. Another is the legalization of abortion. Still another is the discontinuance of transracial adoptions. Finally the societal acceptance of single parenthood has altered the supply and demand balance. No one can predict with any degree of certainty what the future portends in adoption practice.

There are comparable themes of loss for all parties associated with adoption. For birth parents, the major issue is the loss of a child and lack of information about his/her subsequent development. For the adoptive parent, the experience of fantasied loss related to reproduction is painful and needs sensitive attending to by the spouse and/or professionals. For the adoptee, the loss of birth parents and dealing with rejection may be exacerbated if sufficient background information is not provided.

On the issue of the search, we recommend an honest, open approach that will allow the adoptee to consider the multitude of factors he/she must consider and to allow the final decision to rest with the child. Parents must be careful not to impose their own views in either direction. A comment such as "after all, we have done for you, you want to seek out your birth parents" is really unproductive. Likewise, a comment like "I don't blame you for wanting to seek out your birth parents—if I were adopted, I would want to seek them out" doesn't give the child much of an opportunity to make the choice himself or herself. If it truly is a decision to be made by the adoptee, the parents must not impose his or her own views. That is why we strongly urge adoptive parents to first know his or her own feelings on the subject.

The study undertaken to examine the attitudes on all three sides of the adoption triangle revealed some interesting findings. For one thing, it revealed a wide variation in attitudes both between and within groups. The study shed some light in an area in which very little systematic research has explored up to this time. While attitudes between the three groups were significantly different along expected lines, these attitudes were not at the extremes, as one might suspect. Overall, the study revealed that people were generally satisfied with the manner in which most traditional adoptions were handled, that despite some level of dissatisfaction on the part of some respondents, there was an overall perception that the system works reasonably well. Additional research in the area of adoption practice is obviously needed in the future, and should be supported by both private and public sources.

Finally, adoptive parents need to develop an ideological stance that will aid them in setting up a family framework that is both functional and provides gratification for all family members involved. It is offered in the form of a contract, not in a legal sense, but a contract of understanding of the mutuality of roles between parents and children. It recognizes both the similarities and differences between adoptive and biological parenthood.

We are your parents, and, as such, we have certain rights as well as responsibilities. We have the right to care for you and guide you through your youth as we see it. We have the responsibility to care for you, feed and clothe you, nurture you through good and bad times, times when you are healthy as well as times when you are ill or ailing. We recognize that rights and responsibilities are two sides of the same coin and that you cannot have one without the other.

This role did not come "naturally" to us, however. It is a role we requested, hoped and even yearned to assume. We petitioned to be given the opportunity to have a child to love, and to witness the miracle of growth. We are your parents through a legal process. Before we could rightly call you our own, we had to satisfy the courts that we were qualified to become your parents. That process distinguishes adoptive parenthood from biological parenthood.

It is different in a number of other respects as well. It is different because the law says it's different, as we are required to prove our fitness as parents to the social worker visiting our home. Further, it is different because people are constantly reminding us of your biological parents, remarks such as "isn't he lucky to have people like you to care for him!" or "now maybe you'll have one of your own!" It is different because we know there are other people out there somewhere who are directly responsible for your birth. We feel something for them, most likely, gratitude.

We feel an obligation to work through our own vulnerabilities these situations create for us because we want to be the best possible parents. This means not adopting you until we are ready—until we have resolved our feelings about not giving birth to you, and coming to grips with our motives for adopting you. We know it would be wrong, for example, to adopt you just because certain children need homes or to make the adoption a "social cause" for which decent people do make sacrifices. We should only adopt because we want to share our love, wanting nothing more in return than what you are able to give.

Sometimes we would like to forget these differences exist and think of you exclusively as our own (which legally you are), but other times we beam with pride over the fact that we adopted you or, more accurately, that we adopted each other. Our love for you has grown and deepened with each passing day, and that is what real love is all about.

But focusing specifically on adoption for a moment, it is important for all of us to keep in mind that the expectations are realistic. While we know we must not expect a "Phi Beta Kappa" (unless, of course, you are one), you must be willing to settle for less than perfection in us. In essence, we must learn to accept both the strengths and weaknesses of each other, and ultimately of ourselves.

Your becoming a member of our family gives you all of the same rights, privileges and responsibilities as if you had been our biological child. We willingly assume the responsibilities for nurturing your growth and teaching you what is right and wrong in accordance with our own set of values and standards of behavior. We will set limits which we believe you will need in life, regardless of the unpopularity of that decision at that particular time.

Above all, we owe you an open and honest relationship. We will tell you the truth about your beginnings, how you came to us, and what we know about your genetic past. We feel you are entitled to this information. We will give it to you to satisfy your curiosity about your biological heritage. We realize that your identity is a composite of both your biological and adoptive heritage and that questions about both aspects of your life are both natural and normal.

As you encounter questions about your biological line, we want you to feel free to ask any questions, regardless of how silly they may seem to be at the time. Do not concern yourself with our possible reactions to your questions. We will not take them as an insult or as a feeling that you are rejecting us. You have a right to have whatever questions you are struggling with answered in a forthright and honest manner. If you should ever want to meet your biological parents, the first thing you must do is to recognize that this wish is quite normal. The second thing you must do is recognize that there is a difference between fantasizing about a reunion and actually going about it. People may be hurt in the process, including yourself. You must be sure that you can live with the consequences of such a search. Then, finally, you must realize that the law at present forbids such a search by most states unless you can prove "just cause" for desiring such a reunion. But the decision must be yours and we will support you, however you decide. It is your happiness which is paramount to us, and we will stand by you regardless of the nature of your decision.

Children of adoptive and biological parents face many of the same quandaries, experience many of the same hurts and respond in a similar manner to successes and failures encountered in the process of growing up. They are developing, changing children first. Only secondarily are the biological or adopted sons and daughters. The differences between biological and adoptive children are important. But the numerous and striking similarities are, perhaps, even more important. And the goals of parenthood remain the same, regardless of whether the child joined the family by birth or by adoption.

There have been many changes in adoption practice over the years, including some that are extremely controversial and, from our point of view, questionable because they have never been tested out in any systematic, empirical matter. Into this category falls the practice of open adoption, to which we have already alluded. But while we question this practice because of the blatant violation of confidentiality and anonymity, there may be some room for compromise. It may be time for professionals in the field to cease telling birth parents "this is the end of your relationship with the child—you can go on with the rest of your life, you will not hear from us and we do not wish to hear from you. A termination is a termination is a termination and we expect you to sever all of your ties emotionally, physically and spiritually." We think the time is ripe to suggest a modification of this forever closed approach. We suggest telling the birth parents that while your legal rights will be severed, the time may come when you will want some information about how the child is doing and we may want to know how you are doing, particularly in the physical or medical realm. Such information could be passed on through the intermediary, who would then exercise his or her best judgment about passing it along. As long as this practice does not violate the confidentiality and anonymity principle, it may prove to be a boon for all parties concerned.

There are far more similarities than differences between biological and adoptive parenting. Adoption is simply another way of building families, and as such, should be viewed as an accepted way of life. The more people who come to view it this way, the better the opportunities for healthy family growth and communication. The skills, love and caring that go into the formation of solid family ties are the same for all families, regardless of how they came into being.

APPENDIX 1

SEX EDUCATION AND THE ADOPTIVE FAMILY

Constance Hoenk Shapiro
Betsy Crane Seeber

Adoptive families face unique challenges in sex education. Whether they adopt children as infants or at an older age, many parents need support in responding to their children's needs for sexual learning. The authors identify ways for social workers to facilitate family communication on topics related to sex and identify community resources that can provide support.

A doptive families face a broad range of challenges which the recent social work literature has examined. Such issues as transracial adoption, single-parent adoption, adoption of older children, and the sealed record controversy are of concern to many adoptive families.[1] One issue not found in the literature, however, is sex education, which presents unique dimensions for the adoptive family. At a time when young people learn about sexuality from many sources outside the home and learn as much from what is not discussed as from what is, all families must take stock of their responses to the sexual learning needs of their children. In the context of universal issues in sexual learning faced by all

Reprinted with permission of the National Association of Social Workers from *Social Work*, Vol. 28, No. 4 (July-August, 1983).

families, this article will emphasize the unique challenges encountered by many adoptive families.

The issues raised in this article are intended to serve as a
stimulus for social workers as they assist adoptive families. Some
awareness of issues of sexuality may help potential adoptive
parents to be more realistic about future family adjustments. The
workers who help families in adoptive pre- and postplacement
may find these issues helpful in anticipating concerns, recognizing problems, or addressing blockages in communication.

CONTEXT OF SEXUAL LEARNING

Whether they do it well or badly, parents are the primary sex
educators of their children, a fact that is finally gaining wide
recognition. Increasingly, the public views responsibility for sex
education as the province of the home, religious setting, and
school, with the wider community of peers, media, and other
significant adults completing the circle of influences on sexual
learning.

This article deals with the primary locus of the home and
addresses some critical factors that pertain to the adoptive family. Throughout, the term "sexual learning" is used in the broadest
sense, to include all facts, values, attitudes, and behaviors that
affect sexual functioning. Thus, sexual learning is seen as a lifelong
activity, affected by all that occurs from birth to death. Messages
about sexuality are both spoken and unspoken. Sex education is
truly education about family life and involves important messages
about parenting, responsibilities in relationships, sibling interac-
tions, love, and affection.

Goals of Sex Education

As important as sex education is for all families, it is a difficult process. Parents are often urged to "get in touch with" the
messages about sexuality that they are trying to communicate in
their home. Many parents find that they do not wish to perpetuate
the values about sexuality with which they were raised, values
that communicated such messages as, "It's wrong," "We don't talk
about it," or "Watch out, you'll get hurt." Instead of using short-
term scare tactics to "get the kids through adolescence," many
parents would like to think about the long-term purposes of their

communication with their children about sexuality. Some of these long-term purposes might be as follows:

1. To enable children to receive all the information about reproduction, sexual responses, pregnancy, conception, and contraception needed to have control over their own fertility, including the freedom to choose whether or not to have, or when to have, children of their own.

2. To help children acquire positive attitudes about sexuality and the ability to establish trusting relationships such that they would function sexually in an optimal, healthy manner throughout their lives.

3. To provide children with the kind of living and supportive parenting that would contribute to their abilities to be good parents themselves later if they should choose that role.

Although attention to their children's sexual learning is important to all parents, it remains a difficult area for many reasons. Lacking experience in their youth with open communications about sexuality at home, most parents report feeling ill at ease with the topic and doubtful of their ability to help their children combat what they correctly perceive as strong cultural and peer pressure toward premature sexual activity. Many parents report confusion regarding the values they communicate.[2] Frequently having left behind the values about sexuality with which they were raised and gradually having evolved new sexual values, parents report feeling tension betwen the two sets of values and an inability to work out some sense of appropriate values to teach their children. All too often the result is silence about an area in which there is great need for parental guidance, given the constant flow of sex-related messages coming at children from the world around them. The messages conveyed from numerous sources are, in most cases, the opposite of what parents really want to communicate.

Given the importance of family sex education and the difficulty in dealing with it that most parents seem to feel, what is so special about the adoptive family? What issues are important for children adopted as infants and for children adopted at an older age? What barriers to family communication must be overcome to promote optimal sexual learning? How can such barriers be dealt with in the contexts of home and community? This article will respond to these concerns in an effort to alert helping professionals to the impact of sexual issues on adoptive family members.

COMMUNICATION IN THE ADOPTIVE FAMILY

Infertility

Communication in adoptive families is affected by several factors as parents strive to promote sexual learning for their children. Infertility is often the catalyst that causes a couple to adopt. However, many infertile individuals move precipitously from receiving the diagnosis of infertility to adoption without resolving their feelings about their inability to bear children. For these individuals, the sexual learning needs of their adopted child may reactivate certain dilemmas regarding the parents' feelings about their own sexuality. Unresolved feelings of inadequacy, a preoccupation with procreation, and a conviction that privacy about sexual issues is desirable are possible responses in infertile adoptive parents.

As a child begins to grow, one way that parents can help with sexual learning is to familiarize the child with the names of bodily parts and to acknowledge that there are physiological differences between males and females and between adults and children. This usually requires that the parent take the initiative in teaching, which may be difficult for infertile adoptive parents whose own sense of sexual adequacy may still be tenuous. As children continue to mature, they need to perceive their parents as approachable on sexual issues. Parents who have communicated a reluctance to talk about sex may have the effect of stifling a child's questions and may also be unable to perceive unspoken concerns of the child. Parents who have not come to terms with their own sexuality may have special difficulty helping their child with overt demonstrations of sexual curiosity. Likewise, as adopted children reach puberty, their infertile parents may find themselves reacting with a variety of responses to their child's presumed fertility. Hope, pride, anxiety, and jealousy are common responses that parents must understand with respect to the special impact that lack of fertility has had on their lives.

Certain of parents' attitudes may have been shaped by their experience of infertility. If their hopes of bearing a child are still unresolved, adoptive parents may carry with them the conviction that the primary motivation for sexual intercourse is procreation. Such a preoccupation with the effort to conceive makes it awkward for parents to communicate to their children that sexual activity is engaged in for pleasure as well as for procreation. Abortion is an issue to which infertile individuals may have a strong reaction. Both because of their anger at women conceiving children they are not ready to raise and because of their view that pregnancy is a highly desirable state, infertile individuals need to understand how their attitudes on abortion originate. If an adopted child should become pregnant (or impregnate a partner) the parents must be aware that their attitudes on abortion will greatly influence the child's perspective on options available with regard to the unintended pregnancy.

'Bad Blood'

The colloquial term "bad blood" refers to parents' often suppressed fear that their adopted child is destined to repeat the real or imagined mistakes of the birth parents. Such gnawing apprehensions, if not confronted and dealt with openly by the adoptive parents, may have repercussions in their roles as sex educators. When the child is young, parents may be unduly upset by masturbation or sex play. Rather than treating such occurrences as opportunities to initiate discussion about bodily parts and feelings, parents may stifle such activity out of fear that it indicates a hereditary proclivity toward precocious sexuality. Parents' responses to such sexual exploration of self and others can greatly shape the child's emerging image of him- or herself as a sexual person.

Just as adoptive parents may fail to make use of "teachable moments" in exploring their children's concerns about sexuality, they may also be hesitant to give information when the child reaches an appropriate age. Such hesitation may be rooted in the concern that heredity will outweigh environment and cause their child to experiment with promiscuous behavior if he or she possesses the information. This same concern may be magnified during adolescence when the young person's physiological capacity to conceive or impregnate makes the consequences of sexual activity particularly serious.

Whether adopted or not, adolescents crave factual information on which to make decisions and build life values. However, adopted children, in an effort to piece together their identities, may question their adoptive parents about the sexual practices of the birth parents. Although ostensibly trying to be non-judgmental toward the birth parents, the adoptive parents may actually harbor anger or resentment. Such feelings may be rooted in their attitudes toward unplanned pregnancy, poor prenatal care, or, if the adoptive parents are infertile, the ease with which the birth parents conceived. Such unresolved feelings can interfere with the way in which parents help adopted children come to terms with their own values about sexuality.

Maturation

Another factor that has the potential to affect ease of communication about sexual issues is the child's rate of maturation. If puberty occurs for an adopted child several years earlier or later than it did for the parent of the same sex, that parent may need to make an extra effort to adapt to the child's maturational pace. By the same token, a similarity in achieving maturational milestones may forge stronger bonds. In either case, parents must be especially sensitive to the anticipated onset of puberty so they can discuss seminal emissions and menstruation with their children before the occurrence of these otherwise bewildering physiological events.

CONCERNS OF ADOPTED CHILDREN

Children adopted as infants may have concerns about sexuality that are more complex than those of their unadopted peers. Parents who anticipate these concerns can be responsive to the child's need for information, as well as alert to the feelings aroused in the adoptive parents by their child's curiosity about the birth parents.

How Was I Born?

One of the first ways in which a child begins to inquire about sexual matters revolves around his or her birth. For one's biological child, answers to questions usually contain information about conception, pregnancy, and childbirth. The levels of detail provided by the parents will vary with the children's ages and the parents' willingness to be open about their sexuality. For the adopted child, however, the parent may respond with information on how the child came to be adopted and miss altogether the opportunity to respond to the child's interest in sex. Adoptive parents need to be sensitive to their child's questions about adoption without withholding the kind of information about conception and birth to which children that age are entitled. Parents should not be surprised by their child's occasional unwillingness to accept certain information that does not meet his or her emotional needs.

> A mother told her 4-year-old adopted child that he had not grown in her body, although their biological son, two years older, had. The 4-year-old's response was, "I *did* grow in your body, Mommy!" His parents wisely decided not to dispute this claim, because clearly the youngster's current need was for a strong attachment to the mother and to be identified closely with his adored older brother.*

It is common for adopted children to grapple with feelings of having been rejected by their birth parents. Many of their questions about sexual issues will refer back to the circumstances of their birth, information that in some cases the adoptive parents know, but rarely in detail. The parents, therefore, must communicate their openness in trying to answer the child's questions and at the same time remain sensitive to fantasies of rejection.

> A fifth-grade adopted girl had been withdrawn and preoccupied for a week. Gently probing their daughter, her parents learned that her male teacher had been telling the class about his pregnant wife's bouts with morning nausea. After pondering this awhile, the child had concluded that the reason she had been surrendered for adoption was her birth mother's anger over morning sickness during pregnancy.

---

*The authors wish to thank Jean Teitelbaum, Judy Hughes, Walter Parry, and Lee Ann Parry of the Adoptive Families Association of Tompkins County, New York, for providing some of the case examples and for their helpful suggestions concerning this article.

Questions about Birth Parents

Because the information parents have about their adopted child's background is limited, they may need to help their child grapple with feelings about having an unknown past. Whether children are adopted as infants or at an older age, their need to piece together information about their birth parents is compelling. A daughter will often use her mother's age of first menstruation as an approximate guide for when to anticipate her first period. When this information is unknown, it heightens for the adopted girl the lack of physiological predictability that her peers may enjoy. Relating family data on medical histories is also difficult for the adopted child and can be especially anxiety-laden for a young female establishing herself for the first time with a gynecologist. Information regarding use by the birth mother of diethylstilbestrol (DES), the birth parents' Rh blood types, history of breast or cervical cancer, and any genetic problems of the birth parents is often unavailable to the adopted child. This can create anxiety during sexual maturation and in anticipation of bearing children.

Attitudes toward Abortion

As children approach adolescence, it is common for them to confront ethical issues and dilemmas. Abortion is an issue that is heatedly debated by adults in our society, and adolescents also struggle to come to terms with their values on the subject of abortion. Adopted children may view abortion as an especially painful issue. Realizing that they would not be alive if their birth mothers had terminated their pregnancies, adoptive children may oppose abortion and reject it as an option. Adoptive parents who are aware of their child's feelings on this issue must urge their child to consider seriously abstinence or birth control that is 100 percent effective. It is important that an unintended pregnancy not disrupt life plans.

Differences because of Race or Disability

Some children have health problems or are of racial backgrounds different from those of the adoptive parents. This poses many challenges as the parents work to help these children feel included in the family. The adopted child who is racially or physically different from his or her parents may feel difficulty in establishing an independent identity without the subtle reinforcement of knowing that his or her parents have faced the same challenges. These children may have difficulty in expressing concerns to parents, and may turn instead to siblings or friends for support on issues such as health and race.

Often young children are able to overcome social stigmas attached to racial differences or disabilities, only to reencounter prejudice during adolescence. Teenagers are acutely sensitive to peer acceptance and reactions of the opposite sex, both in social situations and as new sexual behaviors are anticipated. The young person who encounters rejection in dating may experience a deterioration of self-image and subsequently view him-or herself as sexually undesirable. The child with a disabling condition may have latched onto this as the sole reason for rejection by his or her birth parents, thus heightening the child's sense of unworthiness and feeling of being unattractive to others. Parents need to be supportive of their adopted adolescent's sexual identity while acknowledging to their child that his or her peers may avoid a romantic relationship solely because of racial differnces or disabilities.

CHILDREN ADOPTED AT AN OLDER AGE

The increasing frequency of adoptions of older children has created the need for a new analysis of issues regarding the blended family. Children adopted after infancy may come into families and be expected to assume quickly the correct role for a son, daughter, or sibling. A similar dynamic occurs frequently in stepfamilies where stepmothers or fathers may expect nearly immediate adoption to their authority and affection. A major difference, however, between the stepfamily and the adoptive family is that, in the latter, the older child arrives with an almost totally unknown past. Furthermore, the child may have no conscious recollections of previous experiences, and there may be no communication between the adoptive parents and the foster family or families who nurtured the child.

Adoptive parents may have no clues to explain such phenomena as a child's bedwetting, extreme modesty about the body, or conversely, somewhat seductive exhibitionism. A casual family conversation in which genitals are mentioned may evoke acute embarrassment from one adopted child, whereas another adopted child may be extremely verbal about sexual or reproductive functioning and become the new sex educator in the neighborhood.

Previous Sexual Learning

All these occurrences may be disconcerting for the parents. Awareness of and sensitivity to possible previous sexual learning is critical and must include consideration of the following:

1. The child's having received negative messages regarding the body and its functions, which may need to be corrected by adoptive parents. Examples might relate to toilet training, masturbation, menstruation, or nocturnal emissions.

2. A different vocabulary about sexuality than the one used in a foster home. If adoptive parents use anatomical and medical terminology, they should not criticize the child's use of less formal language, but should gradually encourage use of common terms in the family.

3. Possible sexual abuse in earlier homes. The child may recoil at any touch or behave in a depressed manner when sexuality or physical closeness is an issue. Adoptive parents may never be certain about whether or not a child has been sexually abused because commonly children suppress memories of such experiences. Messages about the privacy of one's body and children's rights of noninvasion and nonexploitation may need to be emphasized, and sharing of feelings about these areas may need to be encouraged.

4. Early exposure to sexual stimuli. Such exposure may leave the adopted child with unanswered questions, misconceptions about sexuality, and uncertainty regarding appropriateness of communication on these topics. Being approachable for information may not be enough; parents may need to use appropriate moments for teaching or even ask direct questions and lead discussions to reach areas of concern to the child.

5. Sexual values of adoptive parents. These may be at odds with those of the birth parents or foster parents, yet the child may feel loyal to or be more comfortable with previous lifestyles.

Earlier conditioning might include the following: a premium on openly seductive behavior as an attention-getter, flagrant teenage sexual activity exhibited by foster brothers or sisters, and marital infidelity or multiple sexual partners on the part of the birth or foster parents. If the birth mother had an out-of-wedlock pregnancy, her daughter might strive unconsciously to identify with the mother through a premarital pregnancy.

Previously witnessed parental behaviors such as male and female role models may have a more general impact on the child's perceptions of his or her new parents. If the birth or foster parents operated in a stereo-typical male-female role pattern, this may be how the child views appropriate sex-role behavior. Adoptive parents who behave in a more egalitarian fashion may need, through examples and discussions about what boys and girls can do, to introduce expanded sex-role ideas to the child gradually.

A more serious problem exists if the child has witnessed domestic violence in a former home. A cycle of violence exists in which boys who saw their fathers beat or abuse their mothers are more likely to use aggression to solve problems and to repeat this behavior in their own marriages.[3] Similarly, girls may repeat a passive, submissive style if they witnessed that behavior in their mothers. In a comparative study of abusive and nonabusive parents, all of whom had been abused as children, what made the difference for those who had broken out of the cycle of violence was the "richer network of social connections."[4] The new social relationships learned in the adoptive family will be critically important for the child in adult life.

Individual families have varying patterns related to touching and expressions of affection. The child may have formerly witnessed extreme coldness, with no observable demonstration of affection between birth or foster parents and children, or the opposite extreme of direct sexual contact in front of the children. The adoptive family may have a different style and the meaning of touching may be greatly different for the new child. One child may never have been touched affectionately and may recoil; another may have been overly encouraged to use kissing and hugging to gain attention. Many children have been touched only as a mechanism of control or of punishment.

All these past experiences will affect the child's view of what it means to have parents and to be a sibling. The work of the adoptive family in creating bonds with the child and in teaching him or her appropriate social relationships in the family must include sensitivity to previously learned behaviors. In addition, lack of consistent nurturance will be a major factor in the child's fear of new relationships and lack of trust in the love that is now offered.

Efforts to Establish Family Ties

Parents who have adopted an older child have noted some unique behaviors in the child's attempts to establish close loving bonds with parents and siblings.

During a program on family sex education conducted by the junior author for an Adoptive Families Association group, one mother talked about her son who was adopted as a teenager. The adoptive parents identified a pattern of courtship by the son for his new mother. Once the parents realized what was happening and communicated to each other openly about it, they were able to help steer him on a more appropriate path of caring between mother and son. The parents were more openly affectionate with each other in his presence, making obvious that the mother already had a romantic partner and did not need another.

This couple admitted that, as new parents of a five-foot eight-inch tall son, they found themselves engaged in some behaviors more appropriate to a younger child, such as counting his fingers and toes! Creating family bonds may involve some regression in the parent-child relationship before it can mature into a more appropriate pattern. This son who, the parents said, had such a low self-esteem that he may have felt he was not good enough to sleep in the same house with them, often ended up in their bed! A television in their bedroom provided the excuse for his being there as the evening progressed, but the warmth and security of being physically close with his adoptive parents seemed to be a real need for this boy.

The adopted child's lack of experience in family roles may show itself in confusion about sibling relationships as well. The absence of an incest taboo between new brothers and sisters may be alarming for a parent who discovers "doctor-type" body exploration or inappropriate nudity. Activities with sexual overtones may in fact be seduction maneuvers, may be the only way the child has ever seen relationships of any kind established, may only be a reflection of new siblings' normal curiosity about each others' bodies, or may represent an effort to get attention from new siblings and feel part of the family. Many adoptive families find that prescribing an "open door" policy is best. To prevent possible problems, parents ask their children to leave doors open while they play and to expect periodic checks on their activities. Alternate activities may be suggested by parents when inappropriate behavior is discovered.

Shared sleeping arrangements may also meet some emotional needs of the adopted child. The family-bed concept popularized by Thevenin may have some value to the new lone wolf in the family. Thevenin documents the social history of cosleeping and identifies the pervasive former pattern of babies sleeping with the mother or parents until weaned and then sleeping with siblings or older rleatives such as a maiden aunt or grandmother. Lying close while sleeping may meet some of the need for bodily contact in a way that is less threatening that conscious daytime play. In a chapter on the adopted child, Thevenin quotes one mother who said, "In the case of our adopted child, we felt that extra cuddling and togetherness during the hour in bed was the best way to break through emotional barriers."[5]

OVERCOMING POSSIBLE HURDLES

Parental self-awareness is a critical factor in confronting openly the various aspects of sexual learning that emerge in adoptive families. Parents must acknowledge their own emotions as they respond to their child's needs and behaviors. Honesty in assessing their own responses may encourage parents to seek further help in their efforts to be more comfortable and effective sex educators.

Communication between spouses can be a source of help and mutual support as parents strive to deal honestly with emotions generated by the special needs of their adopted child. Questions about birth parents, fantasies of rejection, exploration of sexual values, and testing of new behaviors can evoke emotions in parents, who would benefit from mutual consultation. Likewise, spouses may find that discussion between themselves can promote increased ease and fluency when talking about the same issues with children. Parents should, for the sake of consistency, keep each other informed about the handling of teachable moments in one parent's absence. Traditionally, mothers have assumed a disproportionate responsibility for the sex education of their children.[6] Communication with each other concerning their child's needs, including the need for information about sexuality, can help bring both parents into a closer partnership on this issue. The single adoptive parent faces a special challenge and may want to consult with family, friends, other single parents, a counselor, or a religious leader about the child.

Parents who feel unable to communicate about certain sexual matters with their child may want to set up a situation whereby another family member, close family friend, religious leader, or teacher may become a resource in this area for their child. Local adoptive family groups can be excellent resources, both for exploring issues and for giving adoptive families a sense of legitimacy about their unique style of building a family. Infertility support groups can provide a valuable forum to explore feelings about sexuality that may have been affected by the inability to bear children. RESOLVE, the national organization developed in response to the needs of infertile individuals, has support groups in many areas of the country. Local Planned Parenthood chapters are also involved in infertility counseling and are sensitive to the sexual learning needs of both young people and adults.

Many parents find that their comfort as sex educators increases after attending a class or a course in family sex education.[7] In addition to learning factual information and communication techniques, parents are usually provided with information about community resources they can consult. Often other parents in the class become valuable peer consultants for one another.

Because many schools have developed sex education curricula, it may be especially important for adoptive parents to learn in advance the school's plan for introducing material on sexuality. If parents suspect that their adopted child, either, because of temperament or painful memories, may react negatively to school-based sex education, they will want to anticipate potential problems. Parents can work in partnership with the schools to provide ease and consistency in the way sexual information is presented to children. Failure to synchronize parental and school teaching can have unsettling consequences as the following shows:

> Unknown to the parents, their adopted daughter and her fifth-grade class viewed a sex education film and participated in a

discussion of topics covered in the film. The child subsequently exhibited highly inappropriate sexual behavior on the playground and in the neighborhood. On investigation, the parents surmised that the film had reactivated certain sexual conflicts repressed by the child following her removal from an unsatisfactory foster home.

CONCLUSION

Sexual learning of children is an issue faced by all families. For adoptive families, however, this issue takes a unique twist as children and parents must search for answers not contained in the literature on sex education or adoption. Sexual issues in adoptive families may involve questions about the child's unknown past, curiosity about the sexual behavior of biological parents, the applicability of the incest taboo, or the impact of infertility on sexual attitudes. When conducting pre- and post-placement interviews, adoption workers should encourage discussion of how such issues might be handled.

It is not only the social worker specializing in adoption who must be sensitive to sexual issues. Traditionally, social workers who are generalists and specialists in other areas have helped individuals, families, and groups to forge linkages between needs and services in sex education. By recognizing the need for self-help groups among infertile individuals and adoptive families, by sensitizing community sex educators to special concerns of the adoptive family, and by recognizing that troubled families with older adopted children may need help in uncovering sexual issues, the social worker can contribute a missing link in services.

Constance Hoenk Shapiro, Ph.D., is Assistant Professor, Department of Human Service Studies, New York State College of Human Ecology, Cornell University, Ithaca, New York. Betsy Craine Seeber, MA, is Education Director, Planned Parenthood of Tompkins County, Ithaca. The authors wish to thank Robert Babcock and Stephen Hamilton for their helpful suggestions.

Notes and References

1. See, for example, Dong Soo Kim, "Issues in Traditional and Transcultural Adoption," *Social Casework*, 59 (October 1978), pp. 477–486: Amuzie Chimeze, "Transracial Adoption of Black Children," *Social Work*, 20 (July 1975), pp. 296–301; Sharon Ann Dougherty, "Single Adoptive Mothers and Their Children," *Social Work*, 23 (July 1978), pp. 311–314; Margaret M. Gill, "Adoption of Older Children: The Problems Faced," *Social Casework*, 59 (May 1978), pp. 272–278; and Annette Saran, Reuben Pannor, and Arthur Sorosky, "Adoptive Parents and the Sealed Record Controversy." *Social Casework*, 55 (November 1974), pp. 531–536.

2. Elizabeth Roberts, David Kline, and John Gagnon, *Family Life and Sexual Learning* (Cambridge, Mass.: Population Education, 1978).

3. Richard J. Gelles, *The Violent Home* (Beverly Hills, Calif.: Sage Publications, 1974), p. 181.

4. Rosemary Hunter, "Parents Who Break with an Abusive Past: Lessons for Prevention," *Caring*, 6 (Winter 1980), p. 4.

5. Tine Thevenin, *The Family Bed: An Age Old Concept in Childrearing* (Minneapolis, Minn.: Tine Thevenin, 1976), p. 141.

6. U.S. Commission on Obscenity and Pornography, *Report of the Commission on Obscenity and Pornography* (New York: Bantam Books, 1970).

7. Sol Gordon, Peter Scales, and Kathleen Everly, *The Sexual Adolescent* (North Scituate, Mass.: Duxbury Press, 1978). ∎

APPENDIX 2

SUMMARY DATA SHEET ON BIRTH FAMILY

CHARACTERISTIC	BIRTH MOTHER	BIRTH FATHER
AGE:	22	25
RELIGION:	Catholic	Methodist
NATIONALITY:	Irish/French	German/Italian
HEIGHT:	5'4"	5'10"
WEIGHT:	110	165
EYES:	Green	Brown
HAIR:	Light Brown	Dark Brown
COMPLEXION:	Fair	Medium
EDUCATION:	1st year college. Top 20% of high school class. Best subjects—math, science. Worst subjects—English, history.	High school graduate. Top 1/2 of class; musically inclined; Currently in army as communications expert.
HEALTH:	Excellent. Diabetes on maternal side. Grandfather died of stroke at age 82.	Good—wears glasses for distance.

CHARACTERISTIC	BIRTH MOTHER	BIRTH FATHER
INTERESTS:	Swimming, tennis, horseback riding, classical music.	Writing, music; likes to dance.
RELATIONSHIP WITH FAMILY:	Good with mother; strained with father.	Distant—parents divorced.
SIBLINGS:	Brother civil engineer. Sister in pre-law.	Brother freshman in high school; Earns good grades.
PARENTS:	Father, 46, has own photography business; mother, 40, is RN; 3 grandparents alive and reasonably healthy.	Father, age 52, retired officer. Mother, age 42, is homemaker.

APPENDIX 3

ADOPTIVE PARENT

This questionnaire is designed to measure your feelings and opinions centering around adoption and the sealed records controversy. It is not a test, so there are no right or wrong answers. Answer each item as carefully and accurately as you can by placing a number beside each one as follows:

1. Strongly disagree
2. Disagree
3. Uncertain
4. Agree
5. Strongly agree

Adoptee

1. Adopted children have a more difficult time growing up than non-adopted children. _____

2. An adoptee should have the right of access to all information about his/her parents, including their identity. _____

3. I think too much fuss has been made of the adoptee's need to find his identity. _____

4. My adopted child and I have generally been able to discuss the aspects of his/her adoption without discomfort. _____

5. Adopted children should be able to obtain adequate background about their origins, but not actual identities of birth parents. _____

6. Even if the birth parent(s) and the adoptive parents know each other's identities at the time of the adoption, contact between the two should be discouraged. _____

Adoptive Parent

1. I believe that if my adopted child is able to find his birth parents, it will change the nature of my relationship with him. _____

2. The agency (or lawyer) which placed my child provided adequate information about his/her background. _____

3. Adopted children should not necessarily be told that they are adopted. _____

4. I consider that releasing adoption information violates the confidentiality which I assumed would always exist regarding adoption. _____

5. I would feel more secure as an adoptive parent if I knew more about my child's birth family and genetic history. _____

6. Telling my child about his/her adoption was a satisfying experience for me. _____

7. Feelings of adoptive parents are not given enough consideration in arguments about the confidentiality of the adoption process. _____

8. The idea of my child searching for his/her birth parents stirs up anxious feelings within me. _____

Birth Parent

1. The birth parents should have the right to contact the adoptee if they so desire. _____

2. Birth parents, having relinquished parental rights, should be free to pursue their own lives without fear of intrusion by the adoptee or the adoptive parents. _____

3. It is a breach of confidentiality for an agency to attempt to get in touch with a birth parent at the request of an adoptee. _____

4. Stronger efforts should be made at the time of an adoptive placement to obtain as much genetic and background information from birth parent as possible. _____

5. After birth parents relinquish legal custody of the adoptee, they should not expect to become part of that child's life at a later date. _____

Sealed Records

1. Any person who is part of the adoptive process should have the right of access to sealed records containing confidential information about the adoption. _____

2. I would be in favor of discontinuing the agency practice (where it exists) of destroying confidential information about an adoptee after a certain number of years following the adoption. _____

3. I like the idea of a registry for those adoptees and birth parents who would like to contact each other. _____

4. Sealed records procedures violate the constitutional right of an adoptee to have access to information. _____

5. If adoptees were given sufficient non-identifying information about the birth parents and their adoption, this would probably satisfy most of the potential searchers. _____

6. I think that adoption records should be permanently sealed, with no exceptions. _____

7. I think that birth parents and adoptees who search for each other are generally more unhappy about the adoption than those who do not search. _____

8. Responsibility for releasing adoption records should rest only with the courts on a case-by-case basis. _____

9. Media accounts of "the search" generally give a distorted account of what might occur, should an adoptee and birth parent meet. _____

Miscellaneous

1. How would you refer to the people who gave birth to the adoptee? Rank in order of preference from most preferred to least preferred:

a. original parents _____

b. biological parents _____

c. birth parents _____

d. genetic parents _____

e. natural parents _____

f. other (list) _____

2. Since most courts will only allow the unsealing of records for showing of "good cause," what do you consider "good cause"? Rank the following in order of most important to least important:

a. medical reasons _____

b. psychological reasons; i.e., feelings of loss, identity confusion, hurt over being given up _____

c. desiring more information about blood lines _____

d. curiosity _____

e. other (list) _____

3. To what extent do you believe that opening up adoption records would result in a larger number of people requesting background information? (Place an "X" at any point on the continuum.)

Considerable	To an appreciable extent	Neutral	Minimally	Not at all

What are your reasons for your answer?

1. If adoption records become uniformly unsealed, what effect do you feel this would have on the birth parents? On the adoptee? On the relationship between the adoptee and the adoptive parents?

2. What do you feel might motivate an adoptee to search for the birth parents? Could it have anything to do with his feelings about being adopted? In what ways?

3. You receive a letter from a woman who has been searching for a child which she placed for adoption. She feels that your adopted child may be the one she seeks, and she has convincing evidence to support this belief. She asks your permission to see you and then to contact the child. How would you react to this situation? What would your feelings be?

4. Are there any circumstances under which you feel that adoption records should be opened? Why or why not? List circumstances. Who should make decisions regarding unsealing records (i.e., courts, adoption agencies)?

APPENDIX 4

BIRTH PARENTS

This questionnaire is designed to measure your feelings and opinions centering around adoption and the sealed records controversy. It is not a test, so there are no right or wrong answers. Answer each item as carefully and accurately as you can by placing a number beside each one as follows:

1. Strongly disagree
2. Disagree
3. Uncertain
4. Agree
5. Strongly agree

Birth Parent

1. The birth parents should have the right to contact the adoptee if they so desire. _____

2. Releasing information without consent of the birth parents would be a breach of the confidentiality which I assumed would always exist regarding the adoption. _____

3. There are some circumstances in which it is all right for an agency to contact a birth parent on behalf of the adoptee. _____

4. Birth parents, having relinquished parental rights and responsibilities, should be free to pursue their own lives without fear of intrusion by the adoptee or the adoptive parents. _____

5. Birth parents who try to find previously-placed children are generally dissatisfied with their lives. _____

6. I would like to be contacted if my relinquished child expressed an interest in contacting me. _____

Adoptee

1. Adopted children should have the right of access to all information about the birth parents, including their identities. _____

2. I think too much fuss has been made of the adoptee's need to find his identity. _____

3. I feel that I provided a sufficient amount of family and genetic background to the adoption agency (or lawyer) to satisfy the adoptee and adoptive parents. _____

4. Adopted children should be able to obtain adequate information about their origins, but not actual identities of birth parents. _____

5. An adoptee should have the right to make contact with the birth parents if he/she so desires. _____

Adoptive Parent

1. An adoptive parent should have access to any information he needs about the birth parents if it becomes necessary for health reasons. _____

2. The effect of a reunion between a birth parent and an adoptee would be damaging to the adoptive parent-child relationship. _____

3. Adoptive parents' rights have heretofore been given too much weight in the argument over confidentiality of information about the adoptive placement. _____

4. Birth parents should consider the feelings of the adoptive parents before making contact with the adoptee. _____

5. Adoptive parents should not view the adoptee's inquiry about birth parents as a rejection of them (the adoptive parents). _____

Sealed Records

1. Any person who is part of the adoption process should have the right of access to sealed records containing confidential information about the adoption. _____

2. I would be in favor of discontinuing the agency practice (where it exists) of destroying confidential information about an adoptee after a certain number of years following the adoption. _____

3. I like the idea of a registry for those adoptees and birth parents who would like to contact each other. _____

4. Sealed record procedures violate the constitutional right of an adoptee to have access to information. _____

5. If adoptees were given sufficient non-identifying information about the birth parents and the adoption, this would probably satisfy most of the potential searchers. _____

6. I think that adoption records should be permanently sealed, with no exceptions. _____

7. Adoptees who search for birth parents are generally more unhappy about being adopted than those who do not search. _____

8. Responsibility for releasing adoption records should rest only with the courts on a case-by-case basis. _____

9. Media accounts of "the search" usually give a distorted account of what might occur should an adoptee and birth parent meet. _____

Miscellaneous

1. Since most courts will only allow the unsealing of records for showing of "good cause," what do you consider "good cause"? Rank the following in order of most important to least important:

    a. medical reasons _____

    b. psychological reasons; i.e., feelings of loss, identity confusion, hurt over being given up _____

    c. desiring more information about blood lines _____

    d. curiosity _____

    e. other (list) _____

2. How would you refer to the people who gave birth to the adoptee? Rank in order of preference from most preferred to least preferred:

    a. original parents   _____

    b. biological parents   _____

    c. birth parents   _____

    d. genetic parents   _____

    e. natural parents   _____

    f. other (list) _____

3. To what extent do you believe that opening up adoption records would result in a larger number of people requesting background information? (Place an "X" at any point on the continuum.)

Considerable	To an appreciable extent	Neutral	Minimally	Not at all

1. Are there any circumstances under which you feel that adoption records should be opened? Why or why not? List circumstances. Who should make decisions regarding unsealing the records (i.e., courts, adoption agencies)?

2. The telephone rings. You answer it, and the person on the other end says that he feels he may be the child to which you gave birth 21 years ago today and subsequently placed for adoption. How would you cope with this situation? What kinds of feelings do you think you would experience?

3. If adoption records become uniformly unsealed, what effect do you feel this would have on the birth parents? On the adoptee? On the relationship between the adoptee and the adoptive parents?

4. What do you feel might motivate a birth parent to search for the adoptee? Could it have anything to do with how the birth parent feels about the adoption? In what ways?

APPENDIX 5

ADOPTEE

This questionnaire is designed to measure your feelings and opinions centering around adoption and the sealed records controversy. It is not a test, so there are no right or wrong answers. Answer each item as carefully and accurately as you can by placing a number beside each one as follows:

1. Strongly disagree
2. Disagree
3. Uncertain
4. Agree
5. Strongly agree

Adoption

1. I have experienced pain in my life because I am adopted. _____

2. My parents were sensitive to my needs about matters pertaining to my adoption. _____

3. I think adoptees have a greater sense of gratitude to their parents than non-adoptees. _____

4. The agency (or lawyer) that placed me provided my family with adequate background information. _____

5. Adoptees have a more difficult time developing their identity than non-adoptees. _____

6. Up to the present time, I would say that my life has been satisfying. _____

7. The fact of my adoption has never made me feel different from other people. _____

8. My parents were comfortable (not anxious) in discussing adoption with me. _____

9. In general, my relationship with my adoptive parents has been a positive one. _____

10. For the most part, I find myself wishing that I were a non-adoptee. _____

Birth Parents

1. I would like to be contacted if my birth parent(s) expressed interest in meeting me. _____

2. Birth parents should have the right to contact the adoptee if they so desire. _____

3. Giving names and locations of birth parents without their consent would violate the confidentiality which existed during the original adoption process. _____

4. Birth parents should be free to pursue their own lives without fear of intrusion by the adoptee or the adoptive parents. _____

5. Non-identifying information about birth parents which is given to the adoptee does not violate rules of confidentiality. _____

Adoptive Parents

1. Adoptive parents should not view the adolescent's curiosity regarding birth parents as a rejection of them (the adoptive parents). _____

2. Adoptive parents would feel more secure if they know the birth parents can never find the adoptee. _____

3. Adoptive parents have just as much right to obtain identifying information about the adoption as do birth parents and adoptees. _____

4. Adoptive parents' rights have heretofore been given too much weight in arguments about the confidentiality of the adoption process. _____

Sealed Records

1. Any person who is part of the adoption process should have the right of access to sealed records containing confidential information about the adoption. _____

2. I would be in favor of discontinuing the agency practice (where it exists) of destroying confidential information about an adoptee after a certain number of years following the adoption. _____

3. I like the idea of a registry for those adoptees and birth parents who would like to contact each other. _____

4. Sealed record procedures violate the constitutional right of an adoptee to have access to information. _____

5. If adoptees were given sufficient non-identifying information about the birth parents and the adoption, this would probably satisfy most of the potential searchers. _____

6. I think that adoption records should be permanently sealed, with no exceptions. _____

7. Adoptees who search for birth parents are generally more unhappy about being adopted than those who do not search. _____

8. Responsibility for releasing adoption records should rest only with the courts on a case-by-case basis. _____

9. Media accounts of "the search" usually give a distorted account of what might occur should an adoptee and birth parent meet. _____

Miscellaneous

1. How would you refer to the people who gave birth to the adoptee? Rank in order of preference from most preferred to least preferred:

    a. original parents _____

    b. biological parents _____

    c. birth parents _____

    d. genetic parents   _____

    e. natural parents   _____

    f. other (list) _____

2. Since most courts will only allow the unsealing of records for showing of "good cause," what do you consider "good cause"? Rank the following in order of most important to least important:

    a. medical reasons   _____

    b. psychological reasons; i.e., feelings of loss, identity confusion, hurt over being given up   _____

    c. desiring more information about blood lines   _____

    d. curiosity   _____

    e. other (list) _____

3. To what extent do you believe that opening up adoption records would result in a larger number of people requesting background information? (Place an "X" at any point on the continuum.)

Considerable	To an appreciable extent	Neutral	Minimally	Not at all

What are your reasons for your answer? _____

1. Are there any circumstances under which you feel that adoption records should be opened? Why or why not? List circumstances. Who should make decisions regarding unsealing records (i.e., courts, adoption agencies)?

2. You are celebrating your birthday with your family. There is a knock on the door. The person standing there says that she gave birth to a child on this date of your birth year whom she subsequently placed for adoption. She feels that you may be that child. How would you react to this announcement? What feelings do you think you would have toward this woman?

3. If adoption records become uniformly unsealed, what effect do you feel this would have on the birth parents? On the adoptee? On the relationship between the adoptee and the adoptive parents?

4. What do you feel might motivate an adoptee to search for the birth parents? Could it have anything to do with his/her feelings about being adopted? In what ways?

5. One final question, which has to do with fantasies of birth parents. Do you have any fantasies about either or both of them, either in terms of looks, talents, or what you think they may think of you. Do you think of both birth parents, only the mother or the father as well, or one more than the other. (This is an area where there really isn't much research, so your answer would be quite valuable.)

BIBLIOGRAPHY

Aichhorn, August. *Wayward Youth* (New York: The Viking Press, Inc., (1935).

Anderson, C. Wilson. "The Sealed Record in Adoption Controversy." *Social Service Review*, 51, 2 (March, 1977).

Ansfield, Joseph. *The Adopted Child*. Springfield, Illinois: Charles C. Thomas Publishers, 1971.

Anthony, James. "The Reactions of Adolescents and Their Behavior." *Adolescence: Psychosocial Perspectives*. Caplan and Lebovici, eds. New York: Basic Books, Inc.

Aumend, Sue A. and Barrett, M. C. "Self-Concept and Attitudes Toward Adoption: A Comparison of Searching and Non-searching Adult Adoptees." *Child Welfare*, 63 (May-June, 1984).

Bernard, Viola. "The Application of Psychoanalysis to the Adoption Agency." *Psychoanalysis and Social Work*, Marcel Heiman, ed. New York: International Universities Press, Inc., 1953.

Bettelheim, Bruno. "What Adoption Means To A Child." *Ladies Home Journal* October, 1970.

Biskind, Sylvia. "The Group Method in Services to Adoptive Families." *Child Welfare*, 45, 10 (December, 1969).

Bronson, *The Law of Adoption*, 22 Colum. L. Rev. 332 (1922).

Browning, L. I. "A Private Agency Looks at the End Results of Adoption." *Child Welfare*, 21 (January, 1942), 3–5.

Burke, Carolyn. "Adult Adoptee's Constitutional Right To Know His Origins." *Southern California Law Review*, 48 (May, 1975).

Chestang, Leon. "The Dilemma of Biracial Adoption." *Social Work*, 17, 3 (May, 1972).

Child Welfare League of America, *Standards For Adoption Service*: New York: Child Welfare League of America, 1976.

Clothier, Florence. "The Psychology Of The Adopted Child." *Mental Hygiene*, 27 (1943).

Dalsheimer, Babette. "Adoption Runs in My Family." *Ms.*, 2, No. 2 (1973).

Elonen, Anne and Schwartz, Edward. "A Longitudinal Study of the Emotional, Social and Academic Functioning of Adopted Children." *Child Welfare*, 48 (1969).

Erikson, Erik H. *Childhood and Society;* New York: Norton & Co., Inc. (1950).

_____. "Growth and Crises of the 'Healthy Personality.' " *Personality in Nature, Society and Culture.* Kluckhohn and Murray, eds. New York: Alfred A. Knopf, 1959.

Fischer, Joel. *Effective Casework Practice.* New York: McGraw-Hill Book Co., (1978).

Freud, Anna. "Adolescence", *The Psychoanalytic Study of the Child,* Vol. XIII (New York: International Universities Press Inc., 1958), pp. 275–276.

Freud, Sigmund. "Family Romances," *Collected Papers,* V. New York: Basic Books, 1959, p. 74.

Gochros, Harvey. "A Study of the Caseworker—Adoptive Parent Relationship in Postplacement Service." *Child Welfare,* 46 (June, 1967).

Goldstein, Joseph et., al. *In the Best Interests of the Child.* New York: The Free Press, 1986.

In Re: "The Adoption of T.M.M., (608 p. 2d 130, 1980).

Kocourek & Wigmore. *Evolution of Law, Primitive and Ancient Legal Institutions* (1915).

Jaffee, Benson and Fanshel, David. *How They Fared in Adoption: A Follow-Up Study:* New York: Columbia University Press, 1970.

Johnson, Adelaide. "Sanctions for Superego Lacunae of Adolescents," *Searchlights of Delinquency,* K.R. Eissler (ed.), New York: International Universities Press, 1949.

Jolowicz, Alameda. "The Hidden Parent: Some Effects of Concealment of Parents Life on the Child's Use on Foster Home Care." *Source Book of Teaching Materials, Child Welfare;* New York: Council on Social Work Education, 1969.

Josselyn, Irene. "A Psychiatrist Looks at Adoption." *A Study of Adoption Practice,* Michael Schapiro, ed. New York: Child Welfare League of America. (1956).

Kadushin, Alfred. *Adopting Older Children:* New York: Columbia University Press, 1970.

_____. "Adoptive Parenthood: A Hazardous Adventure?", Social Work, Vol. 11 (July, 1966).

Kerlinger, Fred. *Foundations of Behavioral Research:* San Francisco: Holt, Rinehart & Winston, 1964.

Kirk, H. David. "Community Sentiments in Relation to Child Adoption," Unpublished Ph.D. Thesis, Cornell University, 1953.

_____ . *Shared Fate*. New York: The Free Press, 1964.

_____ . "A Dilemma of Adoptive Parenthood—Incongruous Role Obligation." *Marriage and Family Living*. 21 (November, 1959).

Kowall, K.A. and Schilling, K.M. "Adoption Through the Eyes of Adult Adoptees." *American Journal of Orthopsychiatry*. 55 (July, 1985).

Krug, Dorothy. "Reality in Adoption," *Child Welfare*, 43 (July, 1964).

Kubler-Ross, Elisabeth. *On Death and Dying*. New York: Macmillan & Co., 1969.

Lawder, Elizabeth A. *A Follow-Up Study of Adoptions: Postplacement Functioning Of Adoption Families*; New York: Child Welfare League of America, 1969.

Madison, Bernice. "Adoption: Yesterday, Today, and Tomorrow —Part I." *Child Welfare*, 45 (May, 1966).

Maine, *Ancient Law* 10th ed. (1901).

Mazor, Miriam D. "Barren Couples." *Psychology Today*, 13 (May, 1979).

McWhinnie, Alexina. *Adopted Children—How They Grow Up*; London: Kegan, Paul Rench, Trubner and Company, 1967.

Meezan, William, Katz, Sanford and Russo, Eva Manoff. *Adoptions Without Agencies: A Study of Independent Adoptions*. New York: Child Welfare League of America, 1978.

Melina, Lois. *Raising Adopted Children*. New York: Harper & Row, Publishers, 1986.

Menning, Barbara. "The Family Tree." *Resolve National Newsletter*, February, 1982, p. 1.

Mikawa, James and Boston, John. "Psychological Characteristics of Adopted Children." *Psychiatric Quarterly Supplement*. 42,2 (July, 1968).

Nimoy, Leonard. *We Are All Children Searching for Love*. Boulder, CO: Blue Mountain Press, 1978.

Norwell, Melissa and Guy, R.F. "A Comparison of Self-Concept in Adopted and Non-Adopted Adolescence." *Adolescence*. 12 (Fall, 1977).

Pannor, Reuben. *The Unmarried Father*. New York: Springer Publishers Co., 1971.

Peller, Lili. "About 'Telling The Child' of His Adoption.' " *Bulletin of The Philadelphia Association for Psychoanalysis*, 11 (1961).

Pollack & Maitland. *The History of English Law*. (2nd. ed., 1917).

Ripple, Lilian. "A Follow-Up Study of Adopted Children." *Social Service Review* 42 (December, 1968).

Sants, H. J. "Genealogical Bewilderment in Children With Substitute Parents." *British Journal of Medical Psychology*, 37 (1964).

Schecter, Marshall D. "Observations on Adopted Children." *Archives of General Psychiatry*, 3 (July, 1960).

_____ et al. "Emotional Problems in the Adoptee." *General Archives of Psychiatry* 10 (February, 1964).

Schwartz, Edward M. "The Family Romance Fantasy in Children Adopted in Infancy." *Child Welfare*, 49 (July, 1970).

Shapiro, Constance. "The Impact of Infertility on the Marital Relationship." *Social Casework*, 63 (September, 1982).

Shyne, Anne W., ed., *Child Welfare Perspectives: The Selected Papers of Joseph H. Reid*. New York: Child Welfare League of America, 1979.

Silman, Roberta. *Somebody Else's Child:* New York: Frederick Warne, 1976.

Smith, Jerome and Miroff, Franklin I. *You're Our Child: A Social/Psychological Approach to Adoption*. Lanham: University Press of America, 1981.

Smith, Sandra. "An Examination of Attitudes Toward the Sealed Record." Presented to Psychology Class North Central High School, May 1, 1984.

Sorosky, Arthur, Baran, Annette and Pannor, Reuben. *The Adoption Triangle;* Garden City, New York: Anchor Press/Doubleday, 1979.

_____ . "The Dilemma of Our Adoptees." *Psychology Today*, 10 (December, 1975).

Stein, Leslie M. and Hoopes, Janet L. *Identity Formation in The Adopted Adolescent*. New York: Child Welfare League of America, 1985.

Toussieng, Povl. "Thoughts Regarding the Etiology of Psychological Difficulties in Adopted Children." *Child Welfare*, 41 (February 1962). 59–65.

Triseliotis, John. *In Search of Origins;* London: Routledge and Kegan Paul, 1973.

Walsh, Ethel and Lewis, Frances. "A Study of Adoptive Mothers In A Child Guidance Clinic." *Social Casework*. 50, No. 10 (December, 1969).

Ward, Margaret. "The Relationship Between Parents and Caseworkers in Adoption." *Social Casework*, 60, (February, 1979).

Wineman, David, *Children Who Hate* (Glencoe: The Free Press, 1951).

Witmer, Helen, et. al. *Independent Adoptions: A Follow-Up Study*. New York: Russell Sage Foundation, 1963.

Young, Leontine. *Out of Wedlock*, New York: McGraw-Hill Book Co., 1954.

Zelnik, M. and Kantner, J.F. "Contraceptive Patterns and Premarital Pregnancy Among Women Aged 15-19 in 1976." *Family Planning Perspectives*. 10 (May-June, 1978), 135-142.

INDEX